W9-BMP-026

LEARNING
TO LEAD

A WORKBOOK
ON BECOMING
A LEADER

WARREN BENNIS
JOAN GOLDSMITH

LEARNING TO LEAD

ALSO BY WARREN BENNIS

Beyond Leadership (co-author)
Beyond Bureaucracy
Co-Leaders (co-author)
Douglas McGregor on Management (co-author)
Geeks and Geezers (co-author)
Leaders: Strategies for Taking Charge (co-author)
Leaders on Leadership (editor)
Learning to Lead (co-author)
Managing People Is Like Herding Cats
Managing the Dream
Old Dogs, New Tricks
Organizing Genius (co-author)
Reinventing Leadership (co-author)
The Temporary Society (co-author)
The 21st Century Organization (co-author)
The Unreality Industry (co-author)
Why Leaders Can't Lead

ALSO BY JOAN GOLDSMITH

Thank God It's Monday! (co-author)
Resolving Conflicts at Work (co-author)
Resolving Personal and Organizational Conflict (co-author)
The End of Management and the Rise of Organizational Democracy (co-author)
The Art of Waking People Up (co-author)

THIRD EDITION

LEARNING TO LEAD

A Workbook On Becoming a Leader

WARREN BENNIS

JOAN GOLDSMITH

BASIC
BOOKS

A Member of the Perseus Books Group
NEW YORK

Published by Basic Books,
A Member of the Perseus Books Group

Library of Congress Cataloging-in-Publication Data

Bennis, Warren G.
Learning to lead : a workbook on becoming a leader / Warren Bennis, Joan Goldsmith.—3rd ed.
p. cm.
Includes bibliographical references and index.
ISBN-10 0-7382-0905-8 (pbk.)
ISBN-13 978-0-7382-0905-0 (pbk.)
1. Leadership. 2. Management. I. Goldsmith, Joan. II. Title.

HD57.7.B463 2003
658.4'092—dc21

                            2003014045

Basic Books are available at special discounts for bulk purchases in the U. S. by corporations, institutions, and other organizations. For more information, please contact the Special Markets Department at the Perseus Books Group, 11 Cambridge Center, Cambridge, MA 02142, or call (800) 255-1514 or (617) 252-5298, or e-mail special.markets@perseusbooks.com.

EBA   08 09   15 14 13 12 11 10 9

TABLE OF CONTENTS

PREFACE

Now, we need to turn our energy and intelligence into strategies which will prepare our youth better to be citizens of the world. We need to hold onto the memory of how people from other countries reached out to us in our worst moment of need and find ways of doing the same for them. We need to take as a lesson from this horror how intertwined we all are and be prepared to join hands, as people and as governments, in a partner-like way, to address the poverty that robs so many of hope, of opportunity and of health. And we must take the initiative to get to know our neighbors around the world, to dispel myths and prejudices, promote understanding and begin to create human and strategic relations that will enable us all to prevent what happened to us and what has happened to so many families in so many countries from ever happening again.

Peggy Dulany, September 23, 2001

We have written this book in the belief that honest, capable, ethical leadership is needed and possible for each of us. We intend to support you in your journey to become a leader who can meet the challenges that our friend Peggy Dulany so eloquently evokes in her reflections on the tragedy for the United States on September 11, 2001.

Immediate demands for leadership confront us daily. Our cities are in crisis, our communities face turmoil, our political, religious, and business leaders are repeatedly charged with ethical violations, and the world's multiple demands require our immediate attention. Peggy Dulany has it right. As a member of the Rockefeller family she takes her own responsibility for finding solutions for devastating world problems quite seriously. Her call to all people to reach out and create leadership bridges to one another speaks to each of us who is facing this leadership challenge.

In these difficult times it is plainly not enough to limit our appeal to the existing leaders that we have. Rather, we require a higher quality of leadership from *all* our citizens who operate on all levels of our society. To address this need for leadership we must respond to the daily demands of our families, our communities, and our society by marshalling our inner strengths and fulfilling our promise to lead.

Character and the Leadership Crisis

In leadership, character counts. We maintain that leadership *is* character. It is not just a superficial question of style; it has to do with who we are as human beings and with the forces that have shaped us. Our convictions about character-based leadership come from our years of studies, observations, and interviews with leaders and the people near them—their peers, their subordinates, and their board members. We also believe that character continually evolves as we collaborate with others and acquire their trust, gain their commitment, and build their partnership to realize a shared vision. In observing the turmoil of change in organizations we have observed people on all levels as they demonstrate character-based leadership. We have seen them win and lose based not only on their knowledge of business conditions but also on their knowledge of themselves and their ability to win others to their cause.

As we look at ways of improving ourselves as character-based leaders, we find that the process of becoming a leader is much the same as the process of becoming an integrated human being. For this reason, the process we champion in this book for becoming a more effective leader is highly personal. In succeeding chapters, we offer you opportunities to examine your own life—past, present, and future—and in the process we raise questions for you to answer, steps to take, and new forms of self-expression for you to consider in becoming a more integrated adult.

The signs of a contemporary leadership crisis are alarming and persuasive. Witness the changes in leadership and direction in many of our most respected corporations. In politics, it is the same. The mood of the populace has deteriorated and become more angry, cynical, sometimes foul, and in a few horrifying cases even murderous. Those who ostensibly lead us agree only that conditions are getting worse, without providing us with convincing programs to make them better. We cannot recall such a widespread loss of faith in our major institutions.

One of the most obvious challenges facing leaders today is the incredible change taking place due to technology in globalized corporations, media, and nongovernmental organizations. The speed of change calls for increased leadership and greater skill on the part of those who take up its mantle. Our friend and colleague Charles Handy points to a new form of leadership that is in demand:

> The speed with which change and innovation happen is forcing organizations to abandon their top-down processes, and the new information channels allow decisions to be taken nearer to the coalface and quicker.

Joblessness is eating away at the core of our cities and creating a powerful demand for innovative and courageous leadership to find ways to provide employment and to revitalize our communities. Unemployment is at the highest it has been in many years, and the unemployed are facing cuts in benefits. The gap between those who have wealth and those without much hope for minimum subsistence is growing daily. Harvard University professor William Julius Wilson eloquently describes in his groundbreaking study, *When Work Disappears*, the challenges we face in creating stable urban environments in our country:

> Most workers in the inner city are ready, willing, able and anxious to hold a steady job. . . . We need long-term solutions that reduce the likelihood that a new generation of jobless workers would be produced from the youngsters

now in school and preschool. We must break the cycle of joblessness and improve the youngsters' preparation for the new labor market in the global economy.

The record of failed leadership extends beyond our cities. Around the globe, humanity faces three extraordinarily potent threats: the threat of annihilation as a result of nuclear accident or war, the threat of an AIDS pandemic, and the threat of ecological catastrophe. These dangers raise a fourth threat: the failure of leadership to address these crises. Although nuclear holocaust, AIDS, and ecological catastrophe are serious problems, the failure of leadership is in many ways more urgent and more dangerous. None of the other problems we face can be solved without it or be addressed as long as it is insufficiently recognized and little understood.

Former U.S. president Jimmy Carter, when receiving the Nobel Prize for Peace on December 11, 2002, reflected on the current world crisis. He reminded us that we can each choose to be inclusive leaders and continuous learners as we choose to face the devastating problems of our times:

> The bond of our common humanity is stronger than the divisiveness of our fears and prejudices. . . . We can choose to alleviate suffering. We can choose to work together for peace. We can make these changes—and we must.

With these crises in mind, we offer you a framework for developing your leadership skills so that you can take necessary actions to address the demands of our times, as well as the many day-to-day issues and crises that populate our lives.

In our view, we are each capable of becoming effective leaders. The challenge is to confront the barriers that stand in the way of our becoming better leaders. The learning process that is stimulated by confronting these barriers includes the pain of critical self-examination and the exhilaration of taking the risks to reach our goals.

To grapple with your own growth as a leader, we ask you to assess your character and commit to adopting a set of core competencies. In the process, we propose that you look at *all* aspects of your life. The skills you develop will not only enable you to become the leader you envision but also support you in expanding your capacity to live your life more fully and completely.

The true value of this book will be found in the measures you decide to take to further your own self-discovery. We ask you to observe yourself closely, to activate your ability to learn, to reflect on your experiences, and to change the life patterns that do not serve you. We ask you to reflect openly on your life and to assess yourself and your experiences honestly. We ask you to let down your guard, take a risk, and question your life choices.

What We Demand from Our Leaders

This book is about leadership, but not leadership with a capital *L*. The problems we face are too complex, multilayered, numerous, and widespread for a small group of high-level "Leaders" to make a difference. Our vision of leadership is one in which each person who reads this book, who applies these ideas, and who explores these activities can improve her own ability to become a more effective leader in her own life.

The problems in our cities require leaders on every block, in every church and synagogue, in every community. The crises we face in education call for every parent, teacher, classroom aide, student, and administrator to create visions, inspire commitment, foster creativity, and stimulate achievement. The failures of our corporations demand leadership qualities from every staff member, secretary, salesperson, accounts payable clerk, and CEO in order to catalyze enthusiasm, encourage risk-taking, and create breakthroughs in innovation. The future will work only when each of us *makes* it work.

Most of the organizations with which we work are undergoing substantial, continuous change. Merger mania, reengineering righteousness, and downsizing depression grab hold of and twist all who are caught in their grip. Our observations have taught us that no single leader can save the day. The leadership we are seeking is one that is empowering, supportive, visionary, problem-solving, creative, and collaborative. We seek leaders who embody a clear commitment to values, ethics, and integrity. They inspire collaboration, stimulate synergistic connections, support honest interactions, build trusting relationships, and encourage self-management and strategic integration across organizational lines. They link people through dialogue and collaboration so they can intelligently choose the right direction and become responsible for the results they produce.

What do we want from leaders, so that they enable us to meet the challenges of the future? We have identified four demands that stand out from the rest and have a deep relevance for today's organizations. We believe that most constituencies want from their leaders:

1. Purpose, Direction, and Meaning

We cannot exaggerate the significance of a strong determination to achieve clear goals. The leader's purpose must be to galvanize, energize, and enthrall people and give their work meaning and resonance. The purpose has to belong to *everyone* in the organization. The leader must not only have direction but also communicate it in such a way that ownership is created on every level and in every corner of the operation.

2. Trust

Leaders must generate and sustain trust. Trust is the social glue that binds commitment and promotes action to produce results. Without it, you can't win. To trust leaders, to have confidence in them, we need to experience their competence. Trust is built from openness. We cannot overemphasize the importance of encouraging openness and valuing dissent. Leaders generate trust by including key stakeholders in making decisions about the future.

3. Optimism

Leaders need to be purveyors of hope. Their optimism fascinates others because it is so pervasive and powerful. Most of the leaders we have observed do not get stuck on their mistakes, problems, wrong turns, or mishaps. They see their errors as opportunities to learn and change. Their optimism stems from their clear vision of the future and their commitment to get there by bringing everyone on their team along for the ride.

4. Action and Results

The last quality of leaders that we want to mention here is a commitment to action. That is, leaders have the capacity to convert purpose and vision into action. It isn't enough just to have a great vision—it has to become manifest and real in some external way and produce results. Most leaders are *pragmatic* dreamers and *practical* idealists. They step up and take their shots every day, knowing that, as hockey player Wayne Gretzky once said, "You miss 100 percent of the shots you *don't* take."

Many of you who are reading this book may have chosen to explore your leadership potential while not yet serving in a leadership position. You may be a student, a community volunteer, or beginning your career at the bottom rung of the ladder. We hope you will find this book a welcome companion on your journey. We also hope you will engage this process in collaboration with others. Most crises require leadership that is shared and inclusive. Our image of a solitary leader who is isolated at the top of the organization is out of date and no longer effective in dealing with the complex, multidimensional problems we face. Collaborative efforts, which combine the best talents with a commitment to discovering or inventing the best solutions, are the most successful. We invite you to expand your skills by sharing your leadership with others and providing access to leadership roles for your teammates.

We have given a great deal of thought to the need for leaders who can create solutions to the overwhelming problems we face. While it may be easy to discuss the qualities of leaders, describe individuals who possess these talents, and recognize leadership in actions, it is more difficult to be continually conscious of our true purpose in life and use it to guide us in our day-to-day work. Few of us deploy our maximum energies to make sure we live by the principles we espouse. We want to address this deficiency here. Our purpose in writing this book is to create a means by which each of us can translate our ideals and intentions into reality so that we can act on them in ethical, values-based ways that make a difference.

Three Organizational Requirements

This new breed of leader faces the challenges of creating ethical organizations, institutions, structures, and systems in which each person can apply his full potential to invent solutions to seemingly overwhelming social problems. What are the characteristics of these new organizations? We believe the three elements required for the ethical organization of the future are: alignment with a common vision; empowerment of all involved; and commitment to a learning culture that is based on inquiry, integrity, and reflection. This workbook will prepare you with the tools to lead organizations with these characteristics:

1. Alignment

When alignment with a common vision exists in an organization, everyone has a clear sense of the shared values, objectives, and goals to which they are dedicated. This alignment has a great deal to do with spirit and team atmosphere. It is impossible to imagine building AT&T, Ford, or Apple in the absence of a shared vision. Theodore Vail had a vision of universal telephone service that took fifty years to realize. Henry Ford envisioned common people, not just the wealthy, owning their own automobiles. Steven Jobs, Steve Wozniak, and their Apple cofounders saw the computer as a tool to empower all people. A shared vision uplifts people and harmonizes their aspirations. Work in an aligned environment means sharing a larger purpose that is embodied in the organization's products or services.

2. Empowerment

Empowerment means that everyone believes they are at the center of the organization, rather than at the periphery, and feels they make a contribution to the success of the overall effort. Empowered individuals *know* that what they do has meaning and significance. They show discretion and take responsibility and work in a culture of respect in which they can accomplish their goals without having to check through five levels of the hierarchy for permission for each action they want to take. Empowered organizations generate and sustain trust, flatten their structures, and encourage systemwide communications.

3. Learning Culture

A learning, inquiry-based, reflective culture is one that encourages integrity, where ideas and information flow unhampered to each person. In these cultures people are open to problem-*finding*, not just problem-solving. Adaptive, values-based learning organizations find, identify, and solve problems before they become crises. They understand the simplicity that lies *beyond* complexity is the right kind of simplicity, and they shun the simplicity that comes before complexity. They encourage the free and open discovery of ideas and information needed to solve their problems. They are not afraid to test their ideas. A learning/inquiring organization provides opportunities to reflect on and honestly evaluate their past actions and decisions.

These three elements—alignment, empowerment, and a learning/inquiring culture—characterize most successful organizations. To implement these elements, leadership differs from a commonly held model from the past. The new postbureaucratic organization requires leadership that values meaningful interaction, healthy conflict, and dissent. It is not averse to risk-taking; is supportive of learning from, rather than blaming people for, mistakes; and encourages informal leadership in cross-functional teams. These leaders are better situated to listen to the ideas of colleagues and abandon their egos to support the talents of others. They create organizations that are decentralized into autonomous units in which the decisionmaking power is pushed down and middle management is less important. Management's role is then to create consensus on a vision of the whole—and empower others to reach it. These new organizations require self-discipline and emphasize individual responsibility, relationships, ethics, and open communication.

We have designed the course of study in this book to enable you to become a leader who can thrive in such an organization and foster it for others. We have written as though we were working with you directly, as your consultant or coach. We have shared with you interview results and stories about leaders that have been gleaned from our research and our experience. We have paced activities for learning so they will build on one another. We have also allowed room for your improvisation.

This workbook is organized into two parts. In the first part, we make explicit our model of leadership and differentiate leadership from management; we clarify the urgent need for leaders in today's society; and we explain how you, the reader, can apply the activities and exercises in the book to your own life. In the second part, we teach the competencies of leadership and encourage you to engage in self-reflection and continuous learning, envision your future, empower others through communication, develop constancy by demonstrating ethical behavior, and position yourself to produce inspiring results.

Leadership Can Be Learned

Becoming a leader is not easy, just as becoming a doctor or a poet is not easy, and anyone who claims otherwise is fooling himself. But learning to lead is a lot easier than most of us think, because each of us possesses an innate capacity for leadership. In fact, every one of us can point to some leadership experience we have had in our lives. Maybe it wasn't running a company or governing a state, but as Harlan Cleveland wrote in *The Knowledge Executive*:

> The aristocracy of achievement is numerous and pervasive. . . . They may be leaders in politics or business or agriculture or labor or law or education or journalism or religion or affirmative action or community housing, or any policy issue from abortion to the municipal zoo. . . . Their writ may run to community affairs, to national decisions or global issues, to a whole multinational industry or profession or to a narrower but deeper slice of life and work: a single firm, a local agency, or a neighborhood.

Cleveland might have added a classroom, a union, a playground, or a community meeting to that list. Whatever your leadership experience has been, it is a good place to start. In fact, the process of becoming a leader is much the same as the process of becoming an integrated human being. For the leader, as for any integrated person, life is the path. Leadership is our metaphor for centeredness, congruity, and balance in one's life. Discussing our growth and learning in terms of "leadership" is merely one way of making it concrete.

The premise of this book is that leadership can be learned by each of us at any stage of life. More specifically, this book is an argument for adult learning. Unfortunately, we tend to associate creative behavior and learning with the young. It is probably a matter of socialization that we do not ordinarily think of mature adults as learners.

The best information we have about what it takes to be a creative, generative adult learner suggests that we learn best when we are committed to taking charge of our own learning. Taking charge of our own learning means taking charge of our lives, which is the sine qua non of becoming an integrated person.

The act of committing oneself to being a lifelong learner can take place at any point in one's life. By engaging in the activities of this workbook, each of us has the opportunity to make that commitment to the learning process. No matter what your age, circumstances, or condition in life, the possibility of becoming a leader is available to you at every moment. This book is an invitation to start now, to take the first step, and to become a leader in your life.

Leadership talent can also be nurtured and developed at an early stage of life. John Gardner, former Secretary of Health, Education and Welfare and founder of Common Cause, addressed this question as it relates to the education of our youth:

> Can leadership be learned? . . . The notion that all the attributes of a leader are innate is demonstrably false. No doubt certain characteristics are genetically determined—level of energy, for example. But the individual's hereditary gifts, however notable, leave the issue of future leadership performance undecided, to be settled by the later events and influences.
>
> Young people with substantial native gifts for leadership often fail to achieve what is in them to achieve. So part of our task is to develop what is

naturally there but in need of cultivation. Talent is one thing; its triumphant expression is quite another. Some talents express themselves freely and with little need for encouragement. Leopold Mozart did not have to struggle to uncover buried gifts in little Wolfgang. But, generally speaking, the maturing of any complex talent requires a happy combination of motivation, character, and opportunity. Most human talent remains undeveloped.

Gardner's observations about our waste of leadership potential are indictments of both our educational system and our experiences growing up in our families and communities. Because many of us missed the opportunity in our youth to develop our leadership skills and talents, we have a remedial task before us. It is now time to uncover our leadership abilities and to discover those of others.

We proposed a partnership with you in this endeavor. On our side, we agree to provide a program that will reveal to you the leadership abilities you may not have recognized in yourself, to enable you to hone the skills you may have blunted from lack of use, and to provide the encouragement that will inspire you to express yourself as the leader that you are capable of being. On your side of the partnership, we hope you will agree to take on this opportunity with a commitment, honesty, and a willingness to examine your basic assumptions about yourself and your life.

We welcome you to creating this partnership with us. We hope you will value it as much as we have enjoyed creating it for you. We hope to enable you to make sense of the blurred and ambiguous complexities that engulf us. Your success will depend on your having the best vision possible, on generating the greatest trust among others, on strengthening your ethics, values, and integrity, and on knowing yourself well enough to continue to learn and blossom. Welcome to the journey that is leadership!

Warren Bennis
University of Southern California
Joan Goldsmith
Santa Monica, California

1   Leadership for a Successful Future

We need leaders . . . who can situate themselves within a larger historical narrative of this country and world, who can grasp the complex dynamics of our peoplehood and imagine a future grounded in the best of our past, yet attuned to the frightening obstacles that now perplex us. Our ideals of freedom, democracy and equality must be invoked to invigorate all of us, especially the landless, propertyless and luckless. Only a visionary leadership that can motivate "the better angels of our nature," as Lincoln said, and activate possibilities for a freer, more efficient and stable America-only that leadership deserves cultivation and support.

Cornel West, "Learning to Talk of Race,"
New York Times Magazine, **August 2, 1992**

IN OUR INCREASINGLY COMPLEX AND DEMANDING WORLD, THE requirements for leaders have escalated and are infinitely difficult. The game has changed—dramatically. Strange new rules have appeared. The deck has been shuffled and wildcards have been added.

The constancy of change, the challenge to reinvent government bureaucracy, church hierarchy, and business practices, the demand to rectify blatant corruption, the pressure to survive mergers and acquisitions, and the threat of failure through bankruptcy and massive unemployment has led to hand-wringing and head-shaking in corporate boardrooms, church conclaves, labor unions, public agencies, school classrooms, and governmental offices. In traditional American institutions we've looked to the people who manage to save the day. But most of our managers came into being in a simpler time, when all they had to do to be successful was to build the best mousetraps so the world could beat a path to their door.

Leadership Integrity

As we begin, we raise a caution for you to consider concerning the heady experience that leadership can provide. Learning about it, pursuing or encouraging it, can take you on a dangerous power trip. If the purpose of leadership is, as we posit in this book, to take a stand for what you believe and bring it into existence, then leaders must put a check on their ambitions. In the leaders we admire, ambition is always counterbalanced by competence and integrity. This three-legged stool on which true leadership sits—ambition, competence, and integrity—must remain in balance if the leader is to be a constructive force.

If this triad is out of balance and there is a formidable combination of ambition and competence, we are left with a self-serving leader who places personal power above vision, self-interest before the good of the whole. The combination of integrity and ambition without competence results in a well-meaning leader who is unable to make anything happen and takes everyone down a righteous dead end. Integrity paired with competence leads to good works, but it does not challenge the status quo or open new ground. A three-way balance among these characteristics allows a leader to be true to an ethical vision and to make that vision real for others.

Second, leaders hold a sacred trust from their organizations and those who inhabit them. Followers, who are not sheep but are considered partners in their joint endeavor, look to leaders to interpret deeper realities, explain the present, and paint an enticing picture of the future. The awesome responsibility of finding the right path for others and leading them down it requires leaders who are in touch with the real world and able to avoid getting lost in a false image of themselves. They can resist both fantasies of omnipotence and an addiction to power. A true leader bases the decisions she makes on reality and the needs of others. Our good friend Sidney Rittenberg, China expert, business consultant, and author, describes the importance of information to a leader's role:

> Both a manager and a leader may know the business well. But the leader must know it better and in a different way. S/he must grasp the essential facts and the underlying forces that determine the past and present trends in the business, so that s/he can generate a vision and a strategy to bring about its future. One telling sign of a good leader is an honest attitude towards the facts, towards objective truth. A subjective leader obscures the facts for the sake of narrow self-interest, partisan interest or prejudice.

And third, effective leaders continually ask questions, probing all levels of the organization for information, testing their own perceptions, and rechecking the facts. They talk to their constituents. They want to know what is working and what is not. They keep an open mind for serendipity to bring to them the fresh knowledge they need.

Trust Is a Key Factor

Leaders who balance ambition with competency and integrity understand that building trust is their main objective. For trust to take hold, the first thing a leader must do is generate shared values, goals, visions, or objectives with those she wishes to lead. The trust factor is critical. As trust builds, exemplary leaders also reward dissent. They encourage it. They understand that, even if they momentarily experience discomfort as a result of being told they are wrong, this feeling is more than offset as trust increases, and dissenting information makes better, more informed decisions.

So how do organizations institutionalize honesty, given that so many corporations have institutionalized the suppression of it? There is no easy answer. Honesty and candor at the top helps. When executives speak their minds, they encourage their peers and subordinates to do the same. Many organizations have found ways to generate honest communication—even urging employees to make anonymous suggestions, if necessary.

Creating a culture of honesty in which trust is valued is an ongoing effort. It requires leaders capable of sustained attention and constant vigilance. To build trust, we need environments where people feel free to voice dissent; where people are rewarded for disagreeing; where innovation and failure are tolerated. Trust comes not from a particular technique, but from four characters of leadership.

First, the leader has *competency*. The foundation of leadership is built on the belief that the leader has the capacity to do the job. Skill in performing the required tasks and the ability to mentor those who follow is the first measure on which leaders are judged. Second, there must be *congruity*—the leader must be a person of integrity with values to match actions. For effective leaders, what they say is congruent with what they do, with what they are feeling, and with their vision. Third, people want a sense that the leader has *constancy* and is on their side. They want to know that in the heat of battle their leader will support them, defend them, and come through with what they need to win. Finally, a leader is someone who is *caring* and trusted, who is genuinely concerned about the lives of the people involved. Leaders empathize, and care about the implications of all actions and the results of all decisions. Competence, congruity, constancy, and caring—these are the qualities a leader must embody for trust to be created.

The Buried Treasure

One of the interesting characteristics of successful leaders is the way they handle failure. True leaders embrace error. They do not fear failure. They might refer to failure as a "mistake," a "glitch," a "hash," a "miscue," a "false start," or a "mis-direction." They stay away from the word "failure" because to most leaders it connotes something that is terminal and lifeless.

Most of the leaders we know tend to look forward to mistakes because they believe that someone who has not ever made a mistake has not been trying hard enough. When failure is viewed as something to be faced, addressed, and cleaned up, rather than as a threat to be avoided, great disasters can be prevented, or at least minimized. The recent scandal regarding corrupt accounting practices that were promulgated by that failed corporate grant Enron reminds us of the price everyone pays when integrity fails. When Sharron Watkins, the accountant, attempted to warn Kenneth Lay, the CEO, of criminal behavior on his watch, her boss, Andrew Fastow, the CFO, threatened to fire her. How many pensions and life-savings of working people would have been rescued if the managers of this company would have faced the failures of integrity in their own house, treated them as mistakes to be cleaned up, and demanded new levels of honesty up and down the line?

An Empowered Workforce

Good leaders make people feel they are at the very heart of things and that, when they are, they are making contributions to the success of the organization. When that happens, they feel centered and that their work has meaning. Leadership gives the workforce a sense of its own meaning, significance, competence, community, and commitment. Jan Carlson, the legendary leader of SAS Airlines, describes the results that accrue from the practice of empowering leadership:

> To free someone from rigorous control by instructions, policies, and orders, and to give that person freedom to take responsibility for his ideas,

decisions, and actions . . . is to release hidden resources that would otherwise remain inaccessible to both the individual and an organization.

The leaders who produce the results to which Carlson refers are committed to
collaboration. They require everyone to participate in leadership—and "follow-
ership" as well. These leaders bring diverse talents, perspectives, and constituencies together to form an integrated, dynamic whole. They do not stand
above those who follow, but stand *with* them. They are leaders who listen, empower others, generate trust, build relationships, negotiate collaboratively, and
resolve conflicts. They are leaders who are able to follow and let others lead.

These leaders can be found everywhere. They are naturally ubiquitous because, unlike hierarchical management, they are found not only at the top but
also throughout the organization, in every nook and cranny. Indeed, every employee in organizations that are led by these leaders can build their capacity to
become not only responsible, self-managing team members but leaders who
help run the show.

The Distinctions Between Manager and Leader

Given the nature and constancy of change and the challenges change poses, the
key to making the right choices comes from understanding and embodying the
qualities that leaders require in an increasingly volatile global environment. To
survive in the twenty-first century, a new generation of *leaders*—not managers—is required. This distinction is an important one. Leaders conquer the
context—the turbulent, ambiguous surroundings that sometimes seem to con-
spire against us and will surely suffocate us if we let them—while managers sur-
render to it. Leaders investigate reality, taking in the pertinent factors and analyzing them carefully. On this basis, they produce visions, concepts, plans, and
programs. Managers adopt the truth from others and implement it without
probing for the facts that reveal deeper reality.

There is profound difference—a chasm—between leaders and managers. To state it succinctly: *A good manager does things right. A leader does the right things.* Doing the right things implies a goal, a direction, an objective, a vision, a dream, a path, a reach. Managing is about efficiency. Leading is about effectiveness. Managing is about how. Leading is about what and why. Management is about systems, controls, procedures, policies, and structures. Leadership is about trusting people. Leadership is about innovating and initiating. Management is about copying, about managing the status quo. Leadership is creative, adaptive, and agile. Leadership looks at the horizon, not just at the bottom line.

Leaders base their vision, their appeal to others, and their integrity on reality on the facts, on a careful estimate of the forces at play, and on trends and contradictions. They develop the means for changing the original balance of forces so that their vision can be realized. A leader is someone who has the capacity to create a compelling vision that takes people to a new place, where it is translated into action. Leaders draw other people to them by enrolling them in their vision. What leaders do is inspire people, empower them. They pull rather than push.

This "pull" style of leadership attracts and energizes people to enroll in a vision of the future. It motivates people by helping them identify with the task and the goal rather than by rewarding or punishing them. In a lecture not long ago, as Warren discussed the ability of leaders to nurture and attract others, a woman in the audience said, "I have a deaf daughter, so I've learned American Sign Language. In ASL, this is the sign for manage." She held out her hands as if she were holding onto the reins of a horse, or restraining something. She went on, "This is the ASL sign for lead." She cradled her arms and rocked them back and forth the way a parent would nurture a child. We could not have said it better. Hold on to this image as you embark on leading.

Organizations need both managers and leaders to succeed. However, the old structures that exalt control, order, and predictability are increasingly giving way to a nonhierarchical order in which all employees' contributions are solicited and acknowledged, and in which creativity is valued over blind loyalty. In the organization of the new millennium, a new kind of leader is required, a leader who is a facilitator, not an autocrat; an appreciator of ideas, not a defender of them. Vision, communication, innovation, integrity, flexibility, and inner directedness will be increasingly prized in the leaders of the future.

As we can see, there is a profound difference between management and leadership. "To manage" means "to bring about, to accomplish, to have charge of or responsibility for, to conduct." "Leading" is "influencing, guiding in direction, and action." While every organization needs managers to accomplish concrete goals, it also needs leaders to identify the goals and to build support for achieving them. No organization can function successfully without both roles. The danger, however, is to confuse them, to fail to provide for both and to diminish the potential contribution of each. The difference may be summarized by viewing the activities of leaders as those of vision and judgment—in other words, *effectiveness*—versus the activities of managers that focus on mastering routines—in other words, *efficiency*. The chart below indicates key words that further distinguish between these two functions:

Chart of Distinctions Between Manager and Leader

The manager **administers;** the leader **innovates.**
The manager is a **copy**; the leader is an **original.**
The manager **maintains;** the leader **develops.**
The manager **accepts** reality; the leader **investigates** it.
The manager focuses on **systems and structure;** the leader focuses on **people.**
The manager relies on **control;** the leader inspires **trust.**
The manager has a **short-range view;** the leader has a **long-range perspective.**
The manager asks **how and when;** the leader ask **what and why.**
The manager has her eye always on **the bottom line;** the leader has her eye on the **horizon.**
The manager **imitates;** the leader **originates.**

The manager **accepts the status quo**; the leader **challenges** it.
The manager is the **classic good soldier;** the leader is her **own person**.
The manager does things right; the leader does the right thing.

Bringing the Distinction Home—An Exercise

Throughout this workbook we introduce activities that will enable you to develop your leadership skills. This first exercise provides an occasion for self-reflection and self-observation. In the process that follows, we invite you to discover your deeper concerns, perceptions, and wishes. For this exercise to be useful, we recommend that you be as honest with yourself as possible.

Each exercise in this book is designed for you to complete the recommended activities while reflecting on your own leadership. They are also written as tools for collaboration with colleagues. You may want to tackle them as part of a team in which each person responds to the questions and shares the answers, or the whole team discusses the exercise together. If you do engage in these activities with colleagues, we hope you freely choose which responses you want to share with others.

To address the distinctions between leaders and managers, we begin by asking you to think of specific colleagues in your life who are either leaders or managers. Picture specific people to make this distinction real. Next, we ask you to perform a self-assessment, and then to design an agenda for improvement based on the distinctions. As you internalize the distinctions between these roles you can generate a plan to become a better leader.

The distinctions between leaders and managers that we have presented are conceptual. They may be difficult to apply to your life without specific examples. In order to visualize clearly the distinction between manager and leader, use the space below to fill in the names of people whom you know who typify these roles. Look at your own organization, corporation, agency, school, or primary identification group to find people to consider. If you are a student and have not worked in an organization, select your school, an informal organization to which you belong, a social group, or your family.

1. Begin by making two lists. On the first, note the names and positions of the leaders whom you can identify, and on the second, list the managers.

Examples of Leaders and Managers

LEADERS

Name   *Position*

1. . . . .

2. . . . .

3. . . . .

4. . . . .

5. . . . .

6. . . . .

7. . . . .

8. . . . .

MANAGERS

Name   *Position*

1. . . . .

2. . . . .

3. . . . .

4. . . . .

5. . . . .

6. . . . .

7. . . . .

8. . . . .

2. Given your list of managers and leaders, do you see other distinctions that we may not have mentioned on our Chart of Distinctions? If you find additional distinctions, add them to the Chart of Distinctions. Expand this list to include additional characteristics of managers and leaders based on your experience with the people you know.

3. Now place yourself in this picture by adding your own name to the appropriate list as either a leader or a manager.

4. Use the space provided below to reflect on the questions provided and others that may have occurred to you about the people on the list:

Questions to Consider

A. Was it easier to identify managers or leaders? If so, which one and why?

. . . .
. . . .
. . . .
. . . .

B. Did you have more people in one category than the other? If so, which one and why?

. . . .
. . . .
. . . .
. . . .

C. Does your organization or group tend to support the development of either managers or leaders to a greater extent? Why?

. . . .
. . . .

. . . .

. . . .

D. If one set of behaviors is supported more than another, describe the ways it is encouraged.

. . . .

. . . .

. . . .

. . . .

E. Where did you place yourself on the list? Why?

. . . .

. . . .

. . . .

. . . .

F. If you added new distinctions, did new names occur to you? If so, add them to your list.

Because we assume that the wisdom of the group can be greater than that of any individual, we recommend that you try collaborative learning in small group discussions to give you an opportunity to test your perceptions against those of your colleagues. The give-and-take of these exchanges will allow you to clarify your own ideas and learn from the diversity within your organization.

Collaborative Learning

In order to expand your observations of the leaders and managers you know, find a partner or a small team of associates with whom you can share your perceptions. We understand that you may not have a small team available. You may be reading this book on your own or using it in a large class with no small-group facilities. If so, create a study group of your own to include friends, your spouse, significant other, or classmates who may not be reading the book but are willing to discuss questions with you.

Throughout the book you will be asked to work in teams with others in given exercises. You may want to establish a reference group with whom you will work. If that is not possible, invite friends or colleagues to join you in the exercises that are most intriguing to you and for which you would like others' reactions.

A. To begin with, present your revised Chart of Distinctions to others in your team. Come to a consensus on the distinctions that you think are important. If you have differences of opinion, discuss them until you can reach consensus.
B. If there are several small teams discussing the Chart of Distinctions, share the chart that your team prepared with others and see if you can come up with a revised, integrated list that represents the thinking of all the teams.
C. Now, you can discuss the names that each person has included on the chart of managers and leaders. In round-robin fashion, ask each person to share their list. How do the lists differ? Discuss the similarities and differences in perceptions within the team.
D. Explain where you placed yourself on the chart and why. Ask the team for feedback. Did they place you in the same category as you chose for yourself? The team should give each person feedback regarding his own self-perception.
E. And finally, discuss others on the list and come to a consensus regarding the characteristics of the managers and the leaders in your organization. Finally, you may brainstorm what might be done to increase the number of leaders in your organization.

Assessing Your Leadership Skills—An Exercise

From the previous exercise, you now have a beginning picture of the leaders and managers in your organization or team. How do you feel about your own and others' perceptions of your role? Did you receive any unusual feedback from your team? Do you see the different ways in which your organization supports or detracts from leadership development?

To clarify the distinction between leaders and managers for yourself, we invite you to engage in an activity that will allow you to see where you fit on the continuum between leader and manager. The inventory contained in Tables 1 through 4 focuses on the characteristics, functions, philosophies, and orientations of leaders and managers.

On the left side of the table are the characteristics we commonly associate with managing, and on the right side are the characteristics demonstrative of leading. In-between is a scale from 1 to 5 with which you can assess yourself regarding each characteristic. On the scale, circle the number that best indicates your place on the spectrum between leader and manager. If, for example, you seek situations that are stable and guarantee prosperity more than situations that involve change, uncertainty, and growth, you would circle 1 or 2 for the first characteristic, depending on how often you seek these situations. If you favor neither situation you would circle 3. If, however, you are drawn more to change, uncertainty, and growth, you would circle 4 or 5. Think about how you usually function and circle the number that is closest to your true thoughts and behaviors. If you are attempting to gain insight into your own tendencies, there are no right answers, only honest ones. This inventory gives you a beginning assessment of your leadership abilities. We recommend that you use it for reference throughout the workbook and refer throughout other exercises. As you develop new skills and try out new behaviors, your picture of yourself may change. You can then refer back to this inventory and use it as a tool to measure your growth.

The Leadership Inventory

Table 1:   Characteristic Differences Between Leading and Managing

	Managing	Your Assessment	Leading
Seeks situations of	Stability Prosperity	1 2 3 4 5	Change Uncertainty
Focuses on goals of	Continuity Optimization of resources	1 2 3 4 5	Improvement Innovation
Bases power on	Position of authority	1 2 3 4 5	Personal influence

Demonstrates skills in	Technical
	   competence
	Supervision
	Administration
	Communication
		1 2 3 4 5	Diagnosis
			Conceptualization
			Persuasion
			Dealing with
			   ambiguity

Works toward outcome of	Employee compliance	1 2 3 4 5	Employee commitment

Table 2:   Functional Differences Between Leading and Managing

	Managing	Your Assessment	Leading
Planning strengths	Tactics Logistics Focus	1 2 3 4 5	Strategy Policy formation Seeing the big picture
Staffing approach	Selection based on qualifications	1 2 3 4 5	Training for positions Networks Developing shared values
Directing methods	Clarifying objectives Coordinating Establishing reward systems	1 2 3 4 5	Coaching Role modeling Inspiring
Controlling methods	Standard operating procedures Monitoring	1 2 3 4 5	Motivation Self-management Policy formation
Performance evaluation approach	Rewards Discipline	1 2 3 4 5	Support Development
Decision-making qualities	Analytical Risk-averse Rational	1 2 3 4 5	Intuitive Risk-taking Ambiguous
Communication style	Transactional Exchange Reciprocal	1 2 3 4 5	Transformational Committing people to action Persuasive

Table 3:   Philosophical Differences Between Leading and Managing

	Managing	Your Assessment	Leading
Oriented toward	Programs & procedures	1 2 3 4 5	People & concepts
Resources valued	Physical Fiscal Technological	1 2 3 4 5	People Informational
Information base of	Data, facts	1 2 3 4 5	Feelings, emotions, & ideas Things to learn
Human resources as	Assets to meet current organizational needs	1 2 3 4 5	Corporate resources for today & future development
Change attitude	Implements change by translating vision	1 2 3 4 5	Sees change as a raison d'être

Table 4:   Expected Results of Management and Leading

	Managing	Your Assessment	Leading
Defines success as	Maintenance of quality Stability & consistency Efficiency	1 2 3 4 5	Employee commitment Mutuality/trust Effectiveness
Does not want to experience	Anarchy Employee disorientation Surprise	1 2 3 4 5	Inertia Lack of motivation Boredom
Is unsuccessful when experiencing	Deviation from authority Employee resistance Low performance	1 2 3 4 5	Consequences of selecting wrong direction/vision Failure to communicate vision Lack of buy-in

Now that you have completed this inventory, we suggest that you review your responses. Notice in which sections you favor management more than leadership. Does your character and philosophy tend more toward leadership, whereas your functions and orientation to results tend more toward management? Do you notice any patterns?

You might share your assessment with a partner who knows you and your role at work. Ask your associate for feedback about your perceptions of yourself. Is his view similar to yours? How does it differ?

Creating Your Personal Leadership Agenda—An Exercise

When you have completed this assessment, review it to see if you circled a 3 or below on any item. If so, you are behaving more like a manager than a leader. In order to express yourself more fully as a leader, we suggest that you create a personal agenda as a guide for transforming yourself. The following chart will assist you in creating your Leadership Agenda. Using your inventory as a foundation, make a list of the behaviors you wish to change in the space provided in the first column below.

Share your agenda with colleagues and friends and ask them for feedback. Can they support you in changing your behavior? If they have completed their own charts, compare their results with yours and give them feedback as well. Are there common features in the agendas of your colleagues? If you find a great deal of commonality, you may notice biases and expectations in your organization that reinforce certain behaviors and restrict others. Notice similarities and differences in the analysis of barriers and supports. Similar perceptions of barriers among colleagues may indicate a pattern in the culture of the organization that limits the growth or practice of leadership.

There may be many reasons why you identify yourself more as a manager than as a leader. These reasons can become barriers to developing your leadership potential. List them on your agenda as barriers along with the other issues that block your emergence as a leader. We will say more about strategies for overcoming these difficulties in future chapters. For now, record them and then write down the supports that can help you become a better leader. We have provided an example of how to complete the Personal Leadership Agenda exercise below. The agenda you create here can serve as a foundation for what you want to achieve and can support as you progress through other exercises.

Personal Leadership Agenda

BEHAVIORS I WISH TO CHANGE	BARRIERS	SUPPORTS
1. *Not strategic enough*	*Lack of information, lack of skills*	*Willingness to think strategically, with team support*

. . . .
. . . .
. . . .
. . . .

2.

. . . .
. . . .
. . . .
. . . .

3.

. . . .
. . . .
. . . .
. . . .

4.

. . . .

. . . .

. . . .

. . . .

5.

. . . .

. . . .

. . . .

. . . .

6.

. . . .

. . . .

. . . .

. . . .

7.

. . . .

. . . .

. . . .

. . . .

8.

. . . .

. . . .

. . . .

. . . .

9.

. . . .

. . . .

. . . .

. . . .

10.

. . . .

. . . .

. . . .

. . . .

In the next chapter, to enable you to expand your repertoire of leadership behaviors, we support you in discovering effective tools for transforming yourself into a leader. With these tools, you will be able to address the barriers you have identified and find the support you need to change your behavior and to become a more effective leader.

2 Reinventing Yourself As a Leader

The best of all rulers is but a shadowy presence to his subjects.
Next comes the ruler they love and praise;
Next comes one they fear;
Next comes one with whom they take liberties . . .
Hesitant, the best does not utter words lightly.
When his task is accomplished and his work done
The people all say, "It happened to us naturally."

    Lao-tzu, *Tao Te Ching*

WE BELIEVE THAT EACH OF US, INDIVIDUALLY AND IN COLLABORATION with others, can create ourself as a leader.

Because leaders are always originals, never copies, their learning styles vary. Each person has to find his own way to express his leadership qualities. Thus, no single course will suffice for all leaders. This workbook provides multiple avenues to self-realization. Different starting points are honored. Different learning styles are encouraged. Different questions are considered.

In the course of doing research for a new book on the alchemy of leadership called *Geeks & Geezers: How Era, Values and Defining Moments Shape Leaders,* Warren and his coauthor, Robert Thomas, interviewed the late John Gardner. The only Republican in Lyndon Johnson's cabinet (heading what was then called the Department of Health, Education, and Welfare), Gardner was a reticent, even shy man who nonetheless helped create such innovative and durable organizations for the public good as Common Cause. Much to his surprise, Gardner reported, he discovered during World War II that he was a gifted leader. He had never thought of himself in those terms—but once cast in that role by his government superiors, he thrived in it. Gardner explained with unusual precision how role and talent sometimes converge to produce greatness. His leadership gifts were evident almost at once because, he theorized, "some qualities were there waiting for life to pull those things out of me."

There are unknown numbers of people with qualities necessary for leadership who never become leaders because life does not present them with roles that pull greatness out of them. It is our aim to give you the opportunity to discover your innate leadership qualities so you will be ready for life to pull greatness out of you.

Unfortunately, most Leadership Development Programs focus exclusively on simple skills—and although these techniques are useful, they are not enough. While the recent popularity of instant leadership courses is a symptom of our fundamental need for effective leaders, the courses that offer a "quick fix" foster confusion about what constitutes leadership.

Some claim leadership derives automatically from power. Others say it stems from the mere mechanics of having a thorough comprehension of the nature of organizations. Some say leaders are born, while others argue that they can be made and, according to the one-minute manager or microwave oven theory, they can be made to emerge instantly. Pop in Mr. or Ms. Average, and out pops another McLeader in sixty seconds.

In this book we introduce a different path to leadership development—one that twists and turns. Developing one's self as a leader is a day-by-day, lifelong process that is built on continued self-examination, introspection, and soul-searching honesty. As we pursue our goal of becoming a leader, we learn from failures, acknowledge wrong turns, and make amends when necessary. It is an ambiguous process that begins and ends with oneself. Becoming a leader is a process of self-invention, based on imagining and expressing your authenticity. To be "authentic" is literally to be your own "author" (the two words derive from the same Greek root), to discover your native energies and desires, and to find your own way of acting on them. When you have done that, you are not existing simply to live up to an image posited by your culture, family tradition, or some external authority. As the author of your own life, you have kept covenant with your own promise.

Your Authentic Self

We begin with an assumption that leaders are people who are able to express themselves fully. By this we mean that they know who they are, what their strengths are (and how to use them), and what their weaknesses are (and how to compensate for them). Their primary characteristic is *authenticity.*

We are all drawn to authentic leaders. We admire them, count on them, and wonder what mysterious quality attracts us to them. Yet their secret is easy to discover: They are clear about who they are. To become leaders in our work lives, each of us needs to develop our capacity for authenticity. Only when we wake up to ourselves and act with integrity can we begin to ask the same of others. Authentic leaders know what they want, why they want it, and how to communicate what they want to others to gain their cooperation and support for achieving their goals.

As you heighten your awareness of yourself, you may enrich your reflections with examples from the lives of others. In succeeding chapters, we borrow stories about leaders from Warren's book *On Becoming a Leader*. Their comments are thoughtful, articulate, and reflective. These leaders are by no means ordinary people. They work on the frontiers where tomorrow is taking shape. As diverse as they are in background, age, occupations, and accomplishments, they are in accord on two basic points.

First, they agree that their leadership abilities were made, not born, and made as much by themselves as by external forces. Second, each of the individuals we introduce has continued to grow and develop throughout life. We share stories of leaders who emerged in various stages of life, some in youth and some in their later years. Many examples of leaders can be found who have expressed themselves more fully in the second half of their lives—people such as George Bernard Shaw, Margaret Mead, Charles Darwin, Eleanor Roosevelt, Nelson Mandela, Mohandas Gandhi, Golda Meier, Jean Piaget, and Martha Graham are a few examples that spring immediately to mind of leaders who blossomed in their later years.

Our message to you is that it is never too late to begin. Wherever you are in life, now is the time to start your own transformation. Something led you to this book. It may be a feeling inside you that is a recognition that you have a contribution to make, both to yourself and to others. We welcome the opportunity to work with you, and we wish you satisfying results.

Your Inner Voice

Although everyone has the capacity to develop leadership skills, not everyone chooses to become a leader, especially given the confusing, often antagonistic times in which we live. However, every person of any age and in every circumstance can transform herself into a leader.

First, use this as *your* workbook. Put your name on it. Write your thoughts and reactions on the charts and diagrams. Make notes in the margins. Use it to document your journey in reinventing yourself. Engage the exercises to support yourself in reflecting on your goals and how you wish to express who you are in the world.

Second, engage in an introspective process that requires you to be deeply honest, both with yourself and with others. One of the leaders who understands this process is the television writer and producer Norman Lear. He describes his beginning this way: "First and foremost, find out what it is you're about, and be that. Be what you are, and don't lose it. . . . It's very hard to be who we are, because it doesn't seem to be what anyone wants." But, as Lear has demonstrated, it's the only way to truly fly.

To support your initial takeoff, start an internal dialogue with yourself, identify your inner voice, and learn from expressing yourself as a leader. In learning from your own experience, it is equally important for you to listen and learn from peers, colleagues, and friends—but do so without losing touch with who you are.

The development of leaders begins and ultimately ends with you, the one person who can reach deep inside yourself, who can take hold of your desire to achieve, and who can commit yourself to some noble purpose, value, or vision that is grander than your personal advancement. Norman Lear describes four steps he took to develop himself as a leader. They were: become self-expressive, listen to your inner voice, learn from the right mentors, and give yourself over to a guiding vision.

He goes on to tell of how he was profoundly influenced by Ralph Waldo Emerson's essay "Self-Reliance" in high school:

> Emerson talks about listening to that inner voice and going with it, against all voices to the contrary. I don't know when I started to understand that there was something divine about that inner voice. . . . To go with that— which I confess I don't do all of the time—is the purest, truest thing we have. And when we forgo our own thoughts and opinions, they end up coming back to us from the mouths of others. They come back with an alien majesty. . . . When I've been most effective, I've listened to that inner voice.

The process of reinventing yourself as a leader begins with an internal focus. Whether you realize it or not, you already have the ability, the knowledge, and the experience to become a leader. All it takes is becoming aware of your abilities and insights and practicing effective behaviors that express your natural leadership talents.

We begin the process with reflection, not only regarding ideas but also feelings. As you reflect you can discover your emotional realities and the forces that influence them. Reflecting on your emotions allows you to discover that many of your patterns of behavior are a result not only of what and how you think but also what and how you feel. By reflecting on your past and observing yourself in

27

the present, you may begin to see how the decisions you have made as a result of the circumstances of your life have shaped your stance toward leadership.

Here are some ways you can reflect on both your ideas and feelings: You can remember earlier times; dream; let your subconscious imagine; write in a private journal; talk things over with someone you trust; watch yourself with your third eye; and hear or present yourself in a new way.

Reflection can take you to the heart of what you need to do to become a better leader. Often after reflection, the meaning of the past becomes known to you and you discover the impact of incomplete experiences. By completing an issue from the past, you transform your idea of yourself as a leader and allow yourself to express your leadership skills in new ways.

Throughout this book we pose questions that introduce the process of reflection and self-observation. You may also want to share the results of your reflections with others to deepen the process and to become clearer about your intentions. We also suggest actions you may take to revise your patterns of thinking, feeling, and behaving. As you work through the activities presented here, you may discover additional questions to pursue. You may want to follow a different direction than the one we suggest. We hope you will follow your own lead. This is a beginning. Ultimately, becoming a leader is a personal process of transformation. Reflection will provide one way of getting there and staying on course once you've begun.

Personal Values for Effective Leaders—An Exercise

What we value, stand for, and commit to provides the guiding principles for everything we think and do as a leader. In the activity below, we ask you to reflect on your values and focus on what is important to you. Identifying your values will enable you to determine your goals for putting them into practice.

Our goals always stem from our values. Values motivate us to achieve results that in turn reveal what is really important to us. Goals are end results. We all know when we have achieved a goal. It is a real accomplishment. You can clarify your goals by picturing yourself one, two, or three years from now and seeing what you would like to have accomplished by those dates.

We have identified five values that we have found that are held by many of the leaders with whom we have interacted. These values are expressed in the actions, commitments, and concrete, tangible accomplishments of the leaders we have interviewed. We realize that there are other values that we might have included, and we encourage you to add those that occur to you. The leaders we have identified hold these values. They believe in the worth of clear communication, ethical practices, diversifying the workforce, ongoing recognition, and participatory empowerment.

As you review these values, you may find you feel strongly about some and are less committed to others. The purpose of this exercise is to enable you to perceive and own the values for which you will take a stand. Here are the steps in this exercise in which you will define your values and identify the goals that flow from them naturally:

1. You may remember that in the first chapter you created an agenda for yourself that included characteristics, functions, philosophical perspectives, and behaviors that will enable you to transform yourself from manager to leader. Begin the exercise below by returning to your Personal Leadership Agenda in Chapter 1 and use the agenda items you created as the basis for your thinking.

2. After you have reviewed your Personal Leadership Agenda, read the descriptions of the leadership values below and decide which values you hold strongly and which are less important to you. You may find that each value listed is strong for you. You may see that you have other values and decide to add them to your list.

3. Next, identify goals for yourself that are concrete expressions of each of your values. Consider what you want to do to achieve your goals and to become a more effective leader. In this exercise you will be most successful if

you are specific about what you would like to achieve. Goals that are realistic as well as inspiring will guide your future work, and you can use them to track your progress. They will be the basis for new ways of thinking and behaving.

In our view there are five values that, if held and expressed, will enable you to become a more effective leader. In the exercise below, measure the strength of each of the five values, and answer the questions regarding goals that are related to each value. Remember to consider your Personal Leadership Agenda from Chapter 1. For example, if you are looking at the value of "Clear Communication," look at your agenda items regarding directing and controlling others. If "Clear Communication" is a strong value for you, then you might want to set goals that include becoming a coach for at least one other person within the next year, creating a mentoring program in your department within two years, or taking new risks in communicating honestly with a colleague or a friend during the next three months. When you answer the questions honestly, your goals will emerge.

Leadership Values

1. The Value of Clear Communication

Leadership calls for clear communication about goals, performance, expectations, and feedback. Leaders place a value on openness and directness. Through effective communication, leaders support individual and team achievement by creating explicit guidelines for accomplishing results and supporting career advancement.

Strong Value   (**1**)   **2**   **3**   **4**   **5**   **Weak Value**

Questions to Consider for Generating Goals

A. How can I be clearer about my expectations of the performance of others? And how can I share these expectations more effectively?

. . . .
. . . .
. . . .
. . . .

B. What are the guidelines for the results I want to achieve? How can I establish and communicate them to others more powerfully?

. . . .
. . . .
. . . .
. . . .

C. What are my goals in general for communicating more effectively?

. . . .
. . . .
. . . .
. . . .

2. The Value of Ethical Practices

Leadership demands commitment to and demonstration of ethical practices. Leaders are responsible for creating standards for ethical behavior for oneself and living up to these standards, as well as rewarding others who exemplify these behaviors.

Strong Value   (1)   **2**   **3**   **4**   **5**   **Weak Value**

Questions to Consider for Generating Goals

A. What ethical principles do I value most? How well have I done in upholding them? What can I do to improve?

. . . .
. . . .
. . . .
. . . .

B. What ethics are explicitly valued in my organization? How can I be more effective in reinforcing them?

. . . .
. . . .
. . . .
. . . .

C. How can I better support ethical behavior among my colleagues, team members, and others in my organization? Are there significant differences between my own ethics and those of my colleagues?

. . . .
. . . .
. . . .
. . . .

3. The Value of Diversity in the Workforce

Leadership thrives in a diverse workforce (diverse in terms of race, gender, ethnicity, sexual orientation, age, style, experience, and perspective) at all levels of the organization. Leaders are committed to taking full advantage of the rich backgrounds and abilities of all people and promoting greater diversity, especially in positions of influence and power. Differing points of view are sought, diversity is valued, and honesty and teamwork are rewarded.

Strong Value   1   (2)   3   4   5   **Weak Value**

Questions to Consider for Generating Goals

A. What are my goals for increasing my capacity to understand and support diversity?

. . . .
. . . .
. . . .
. . . .

B. How can I encourage greater diversity in my organization in positions of influence and power?

. . . .
. . . .
. . . .
. . . .

C. What can I do to reward the expression of diverse styles, values, and points of view?

. . . .
. . . .
. . . .
. . . .

4. The Value of Ongoing Recognition

Leadership provides appropriate and ongoing recognition—both financial and psychic—for teams and individuals who contribute to the success of the overall endeavor. Leaders acknowledge their own mistakes and recognize the contributions of others to solving problems. Leaders value those who create and innovate, as well as those who critique and support the day-to-day requirements of the organization.

Strong Value   1   2   ③   4   5   **Weak Value**

Questions to Consider for Generating Goals

A. How can I recognize the achievements of others more effectively?

. . . .

. . . .

. . . .

. . . .

B. What are my goals for an equitable system of rewards and recognition?

. . . .

. . . .

. . . .

. . . .

C. What can I do to support those who are critical as well as those who are supportive of my ideas?

. . . .

. . . .

. . . .

. . . .

5. The Value of Participatory Empowerment

Leadership encourages participation in decisionmaking of all those who are directly involved in producing results by increasing their power, authority, and responsibility for outcomes. Leaders encourage teamwork, trust, and regular feedback. In stimulating and releasing the capacity of all people in the organization, leaders increase their satisfaction and empower them to be successful.

Strong Value   1   (2)   3   4   5   **Weak Value**

Questions to Consider for Generating Goals

A. What can I do to more effectively empower others?

. . . .

. . . .

. . . .

. . . .

B. How can I increase my capacity to transfer authority and responsibility to those directly involved?

. . . .

. . . .

. . . .

. . . .

C. What can I do to enable colleagues to empower themselves for greater satisfaction and success?

. . . .

. . . .

. . . .

. . . .

Reflecting on your values and generating your goals is a useful exercise, however, you must go beyond reflection to action to complete the leadership transformation process. Without a firm commitment to your values and a clear intention to achieve your goals in real life, this exercise will be worthless.

Commitment is the missing piece in the puzzle of success. Leaders are clear about their commitments and are willing to declare and demonstrate them through their actions. Commitment is the fuel that drives leaders. It reminds them of their values, inspires others to respect these values, and motivates them to achieve their goals. As you create your goals in the exercise below, choose ones to which you can genuinely and enthusiastically commit. As you share them with others, let them know the strength of your commitment to achieve what you set out to do.

Powerful Goals for Leaders—An Exercise

In the exercise above, you have clarified your values and identified a number of changes you would like to make in your thinking and behavior to become a more effective leader. Some of your goals can be achieved in the short term, even as you read this book. Others will take longer and remain with you throughout your life.

To make change worthwhile, we distinguish between what we can accomplish immediately and what will be the basis for ongoing, lifelong learning. For example, you may have a goal of being more conscious of diverse perspectives—other than your own—by being open to divergent viewpoints on a regular basis. That is a short-term goal. A goal that might take longer to achieve would be to change your communication patterns so that you are clearer and more direct in sharing your expectations with others and letting them know when you are satisfied or disappointed.

In completing the following chart, you have the opportunity to distinguish your short-term and long-term goals. Notice in this exercise that we make a request to specify a date by which you will have achieved your goal. Without clarifying a date for completion, you may lack the urgency required for achieving what you want. We have included an example in each section of the chart to guide you as you proceed. Completing this chart and referring to it as you proceed will remind you of the changes you intend to make and clarify your direction, progress, and commitment. You might want to post a copy of it near your work space to remind you of your intentions. You may also want to revise the chart as you proceed and as your goals change to meet new circumstances.

Goals Chart

SHORT-TERM GOALS (DATE)	LONG-TERM GOALS (DATE)
Communication	
Be more direct in making requests—11/1/05	*Better communicate my vision—3/1/05*
. . . .	
Ethical Management Practices	
Be more scrupulous about the accuracy of my expense report—12/1/05	*In collaboration with my team, create an ethical standards statement for clients—7/1/06*
. . . .	
Diversity	
Be more sensitive to the comfort of colleagues of the opposite gender or of a different race when telling stories or jokes in front of them—10/3/04	*Encourage others who disagree with me to speak up—2/1/05*

. . . .

. . . .

. . . .

. . . .

Recognition

Acknowledge the good work of a colleague at least once a day—10/3/04

Do an inventory of my own accomplishments and create ways to acknowledge others—5/1/05

. . . .

. . . .

. . . .

. . . .

Empowerment

Look for opportunities to transfer authority to others—9/7/04

Create a plan for greater shared decisionmaking—2/20/06

. . . .

. . . .

. . . .

. . . .

Other Goals I Have

. . . .

. . . .

. . . .

. . . .

. . . .

. . . .

Leadership in a Team—An Exercise

If you are working with a partner, classmates, a team, or colleagues, you may want to share the goals you have generated. It is often useful to hear the plans of others for their leadership development. When you and your colleagues share goals, you may want to make additions or changes in your own chart based on what your colleagues suggest. In some cases, you may have information on your chart that is too personal to show to anyone else. That's fine. You don't need to share what you feel is too personal. Perhaps you can pick one goal to share that is not too close to home. We suggest that each person communicate at least one goal to team members so everyone can support each other in realizing your intentions. You can also use this team discussion as an opportunity to get valuable feedback from those who know you well. Ask them for their reactions to these questions:

Questions to Consider

A. Are my goals realistic? Have I set myself up for failure by targeting too high? Am I aiming too low for myself? Can I achieve more than I have projected?

. . . .

. . . .

. . . .

. . . .

B. Given what you know about me, are there other areas I should target for development?

. . . .

. . . .

. . . .

. . . .

C. Have I been clear enough in my short-term goals about what I can do immediately? Will my long-term goals be achieved sooner than projected? What can I do to make my targets clearer?

. . . .

. . . .

. . . .

. . . .

Your team may want to create a chart to show the goals of the entire team. Start by identifying one or two goals for each person that can be supported by the team. If you work in proximity to one another, you can post the chart near everyone's work space, or create a list-serve to share the team goals online and track achievements. A team leadership chart of goals might look as follows:

Team Leadership Goals

SHORT-TERM GOALS (DATE)   LONG-TERM GOALS (DATE)

Person A

. . . .

. . . .

Person B

. . . .

. . . .

Person C

. . . .

. . . .

As you look at the goals for each person, you may discover that some are held in common by everyone. These common goals can form the basis for a team project. For example, several people may have the short-term goal of increasing the times and ways individual achievements are acknowledged in the department. The team may decide to take on achieving this goal and work on it together, mounting an acknowledgment campaign and planning special rewards, acknowledgment lunches, employee-of-the-month announcements, and so on.

You may want to shape a process that tracks individual and team goals in order to record each person's progress. If you do, set up a reporting system that will let everyone know the results for both individuals and the team. If your organization has regular staff meetings, electronic mail, or voice communications systems, you can create tracking mechanisms that make everyone aware of the progress being made. Everyone on the team can then support each other's efforts. A buddy system allows colleagues to encourage each other in achieving their desired results.

Qualities That Support Leadership Development—An Exercise

At this point in your development process, we recommend that you conduct a self-assessment that will enable you to make your goals more concrete and give direction to your thinking and actions. This self-assessment focuses on the qualities that will support you in learning to become a better leader. Through the answers to these questions, you will understand more about your strengths and weaknesses and how you can focus your learning activities to improve your leadership skills.

Questions to Consider

A. Given my goals for reinventing myself as a leader, what are the qualities I bring that will enable me to be successful?

. . . .
. . . .
. . . .
. . . .
. . . .
. . . .
. . . .

B. What are the elements of my style, personality, and skills that will make my learning to be a better leader more difficult? What is it about me that tends to get in the way of being a successful leader?

. . . .
. . . .
. . . .
. . . .
. . . .
. . . .
. . . .

C. As I remember a time in recent years when I learned a new skill, played a new role, or took on a new physical challenge, on what talents did I draw? What was it about my thoughts, feelings, or actions that allowed me to be successful? What stood in my way?

. . . .
. . . .
. . . .
. . . .

. . . .

. . . .

. . . .

D. How, in this recent experience, did I undermine or devalue myself? How did I misjudge myself? What did I draw upon to overcome the odds so that I could succeed?

. . . .

. . . .

. . . .

. . . .

. . . .

. . . .

. . . .

If you are working with colleagues, share the qualities you have identified that you believe will enable you to be a better leader, as well as those that stand in the way of reaching your goals. Ask your colleagues for feedback based on their perceptions of your behavior. Incorporate their comments in the questions above. If you are on a team that is completing this exercise, after each person shares the qualities that have enabled him to learn, have the team create a composite of the specific qualities that were mentioned so the team can see what each person can do in the future to support the other team members in learning to become more skillful leaders.

Specific Qualities That Support Learning to Become a Leader As Identified by the Team:

1. . . . .

2. . . . .

3. . . . .

4. . . . .

5. . . . .

6. . . . .

7. . . . .

8. . . . .

As you examine the qualities above, consider the ways your team and the organization as a whole can encourage each person to express herself as a leader.

Questions to Consider

A. How can we as a group, team, or organization support these qualities in ourselves and others so we can become more successful in developing ourselves and others as leaders?

. . . .

. . . .

. . . .

. . . .

. . . .

. . . .

. . . .

B. How can we support one another in developing our leadership skills?

. . . .

. . . .

. . . .

. . . .

. . . .

. . . .

. . . .

C. In examining the qualities that the team has identified, what were the qualities mentioned by colleagues that I had not considered? Why not?

. . . .

. . . .

. . . .

. . . .

. . . .

. . . .

. . . .

The work you have done here to clarify your goals and identify the qualities you bring to achieving them will be useful throughout this workbook. As you continue, you may want to refer back to your goals, values, and qualities. They are reminders of where you are headed and the resources that you bring to the process of getting there.

3   The Leadership Crisis

*Finding the leader within, our heroic self, does more than unshackle us from
the external leaders to whom we so desperately have held fast. It also frees up
much more leadership talent for the entire society, in every organization, at
every level. This new breed of leaders will be more self-reliant and thoughtful.
These will be leaders who can handle the magnificent uncertitude of our
times, the anxiety it augments, and the opportunities for learning and change
that both uncertainty and anxiety generate.*

Jean Lipman Blumen, *Why Do We Tolerate Bad Leaders?*
Magnificent Uncertitude, Anxiety, and Meaning

WHERE HAVE ALL THE LEADERS GONE? MANY OF THEM, LIKE THE
flowers of the haunting folk song, are "long time passing." Many of the
leaders we once respected are now dead. FDR, who challenged a nation to rise
above fear, is gone. Martin Luther King Jr., who taught us to struggle to realize
the dream of equality, is gone. Winston Churchill, who demanded and got blood,
sweat, and tears, is gone. Albert Schweitzer, who inspired mankind with a rever-
ence for life from the jungles of Lambaréné, is gone. Albert Einstein, who gave us
a sense of unity in infinity, of cosmic harmony, is gone. Mohandas Gandhi, John
and Robert Kennedy, Anwar Sadat, Yitzak Rabin, Malcolm X—all were slain.
Their deaths are testimonies to the mortal risk of telling humanity that we can
be greater and better than we are.

Leaders today seem to be an endangered species, caught in a whirl of events
and circumstances beyond our rational control. In the last two decades, there

has been a high turnover, an appalling mortality—both occupational and actuarial—among leaders. As part of the same pattern, the "shelf life" of college presidents and CEOs has been markedly reduced. In the 1950s, the average tenure for college presidents was more than eleven years; today it's more like four years. Similarly, corporate chieftains' days at the top seem to be numbered from the moment they step up to the job. Superintendents of big-city school districts last two to three years, often citing health reasons for leaving. In local communities, the burnout factor discourages school, government, and neighborhood reformers from sticking to it for the long haul. With leadership tenure so tenuous, it is no wonder that we are crying out for inspired leaders whose integrity is beyond question. The stakes are very high. Our quality of life depends on the quality of our leaders. In our view, it is now up to *you*. If you have ever had dreams of leadership, now is the time, this is the place, and you are the one. We need you.

There are three basic reasons why leaders are important to all of us. First, they are responsible for the effectiveness of our organizations. The success or failure of all organizations, be they basketball teams, filmmakers, or automobile manufacturers, rests on perceived quality at the top. Even stock prices of large corporations have been shown to rise and fall according to the public's perception of the effectiveness of their leaders.

Second, the change and upheaval of the past several years have left us without a clear sense of our vision, goals, or the direction in which we ought to be heading. We need a guiding purpose. Leaders enable us to create one for ourselves.

Third, there is a pervasive, national concern about the integrity of our institutions. Wall Street was, not long ago, a place where a person's word was her bond. Recent investigations, revelations, scandals, and indictments have forced the industry to change the way it has conducted business for more than 150 years. Cynicism has poisoned our business environment. A recent *New York Times* article, featured on the Business Day news pages rather than in an editorial column, reflects the outrage and cynicism that has resulted from our betrayal by American business leaders:

In the bizarre yet lucrative world of Enron's bankruptcy, everyone seems to have a complaint these days. The $300-an-hour lawyers complain that the $500-an-hour lawyers are charging exorbitant fees. The legal eagles from Texas insist that the legal eagles from New York are dominating the court proceedings. Creditors accused of ethical conflicts question the ethics of the examiner appointed by the court to question theirs. The only thing people seem to agree on is that the case—second only to WorldCom's in size—is likely to be the costliest bankruptcy in history. Already, lawyers and other professionals have billed Enron close to $300 million in what some critics say is an unparalleled fee bonanza.

"These fees are extraordinary and appalling, when one considers that most shareholders and small creditors are likely to see little recovery in this bankruptcy," said Andrew Entwistle, a lawyer representing some creditors.

To observe that times are changing is an understatement. Never before have business institutions faced so many challenges, and never before have there been so many choices over how to face those challenges. Public mistrust of the leadership of all of our institutions today is rampant. In a recent *New York Times/CBS* poll, only 15 percent of the public expressed any confidence in big business, and 67 percent believed that most corporate executives are not honest. In a *Time* magazine poll released in January 2003, 57 percent of Americans, when asked to identify what constituted the greatest threat to world peace, cited their own government.

In the midst of these worrisome doubts and fears, the dizzying pace of change has further exacerbated the problem. CEOs appointed after 1990 are three times more likely to be fired than CEOs appointed before that date. And since the year 2000, 77 of the 200 largest companies have ousted their leaders and hired a new boss. These figures definitely reflect the times in which we are living. The rampant mistrust of leaders, the possibility of very serious global recessions, the effects of the 9/11 tragedy—all have created an Age of Vulnerability and a fierce, Darwinian competition for survival.

As we confront the dearth of leadership at this moment we are forced to face the question "Can we do it?" Can we fill the void? What will the world of leadership in organizations look like in 2020? Will the pattern resemble the huge megamergers of GE, Time-Warner, PB-Amoco-Arco, Viacom, and Intel? Or will it look like a small, ramshackle Hollywood model, where groups from diverse disciplines gather together for short periods of time, develop or finish a product, and then, after a spell, regroup? Or will there be some kind of combination, a hybrid of Great Groups working together interdependently, rather than independently under some large, decentralized behemoth's umbrella?

Another dilemma of the future, and one we tend to duck, is what we do with the growing disparities. The increasing chasm of income between the top quintile and the bottom quintile—along with the obscene differential between the average CEO and the average worker ($419 to $1 at last count) is a serious issue. It's important to note that nearly 90 percent of stocks are owned by only 10 percent of the population, with the top 1 percent owning 51.4 percent. Add to that the increasing disparities in education and family services. Should we not be worrying about the impoverishment of a large percentage of our population? Do we have any responsibility for what is happening, or finding ways of remedying these achingly stubborn inequalities?

And what about the important demographic changes that are now upon us? We are thinking specifically about ageism, both among the young and the old. The sixty-and-older crowd is not only living longer and healthier, but according to all reports, it members want to work way beyond age sixty or sixty-five. A recent study by Civic Ventures reports that 50 percent of older Americans (however that's defined) are working for pay in their "retirement," and another 40 percent perform regular volunteer work. The golden years are dead, the report claims. Think of this: As recently as 1960, according to a recent issue of the *Economist*, "men could expect to spend 50 of their 68 years of life in paid work. Today, they are likely to work for only 38 of their 76 years." What should organizations do to retain the wisdom of their aging employees without forestalling the futures of coming generations? And what about the nonexistent leadership of bored twenty-something millionaires?

The policy issues these demographics raise have serious implications. Just to take one: If workers continue to take early retirement (and the average age of retirement seems to be declining to the early sixties in the United States and much lower in all the European countries), and with the boomers in massive numbers hitting retirement in the near future, there won't be enough wage earners to support boomer retirees.

And what about the social contract between employers and employees, that hallowed implicit contract that usually offered some form of loyalty and responsibility to both parties? Roughly 25 percent of the U.S. workforce has been dumped since 1985, and even at present, figure on a half to three-quarters of a million employees in flux every year. What's interesting is that in 1998, about 750,000 workers were laid off or quit or retired, and of those, 92 percent found jobs that paid either more or were equal to what they had been getting. A recent survey reported in the *Wall Street Journal* reveals that four out of ten employees stay less than three years at their jobs, only a third of the workforce maintains the old-fashioned 9-to-5 shift, and the quit rate last year rose to 14.5 percent. It was about 3 percent ten years ago. We figure that the churn of the workforce, that is, the number of workers who are temporarily out of work or looking for new opportunities, at any given moment is between 20 and 25 percent.

Is the high rate of CEO turnover we see today necessary? There's been a lot of interest recently in revolving doors for CEOs. A recent Harvard Business School study shows that corporate boards of directors are 30 percent more likely to oust a CEO than they were ten years ago. Doubtless, a number of complex factors are involved in the diminishing half-life of executive tenure: hypercompetition, Internet volatility, turbocharged globalism, trillion-dollar mergers—you can round up the usual suspects. Reflecting this interest, *Fortune* ran a cover story recently with ten notable CEOs who had been axed by their boards. In fact, boards of directors have an enormous and not fully understood impact on executive failure.

We are curious about how leaders sustain creativity and keep their juices flowing. We think a lot of Gary Hamel's powerful question: "Are we learning as fast as the world is changing?" It is clear to us that in order to prevail in this time of leadership crisis, we need leaders who can sustain themselves, maintain the pace, balance their priorities, and build meaning into each day of work.

How do we keep our eyes and ears open to these nascent, potentially disruptive inflection points? How much does sheer luck contribute, and why is it that we're witnessing this tsunami of senior executive churning?

Today, in the first years of the twenty-first century, we find that the people who can afford to retreat into their own electronic castles increasingly work at home and communicate with the world via computers that screen their calls, order movies for their VCRs and DVDs, order takeout food for their microwave ovens, and bring in trainers to keep their bodies in shape. They keep the world at bay with advanced security systems and refuse to acknowledge what is happening—and the costs of what is happening—to those who lack their resources. Trend-spotters call this phenomenon "cocooning," but it looks to us more like terminal egocentricity. Whatever it is, it is not leadership.

We know that a nation cannot survive without public virtue and that it cannot progress without shared values and a common vision, yet we see no leaders on the horizon who can enable us to restore our virtue and values. America has not had a national sense of purpose since World War II, or among a large part of its population since the 1960s, when, in an unprecedented show of common cause, millions of Americans vehemently opposed government policies. Instead of changing its policies, however, the government went underground. The Iran-contra affair, like Watergate before it, was an effort to deceive the American people.

As the government went underground and the more affluent among us took to their electronic towers, an especially ugly breed of entrepreneurial parasite took over our inner cities, peddling crack not only to the underclass but to the uneasy rich and the bored children of the middle class. Today, Americans spend more money annually on drugs than on oil. The land of the free and the home of the brave is the world's number-one drug addict.

Where have all the leaders gone? They're out there pleading, trotting, temporizing, putting out fires, trying to avoid too much heat. They're peering at a landscape of bottom lines. They're money-changers lost in a narrow orbit. They resign. They burn out. They decide not to run or serve. They're organizational *Houdinis*, surrounded by sharks or shackled in a water cage, always managing to escape, miraculously, to make more money via their escape clauses than they made in several years of work. They motivate people through fear, by following trends, or by posing as advocates of "reality," which they cynically make up as they go along. They are leading characters in the dreamless society, given now almost exclusively to solo turns. Thus, precisely at the time when the trust and credibility of our alleged leaders are at an all-time low and when potential leaders feel most inhibited in exercising their gifts, America most needs leaders everywhere and at all times—because, of course, as the quality of leaders declines, the quantity of problems escalates. Just as a person cannot function without a brain, a society cannot function without leaders. And so the decline goes on.

If it is true that the current leadership crisis is pernicious and all-pervasive, why should we bother to concern ourselves with it, to label it, understand it, describe or characterize it? Why do we need to analyze the extent of the problem? What difference could it make in our daily lives if we were to become conscious of our own potential for leadership?

In an earlier book, *Why Leaders Can't Lead*, Warren wrote that there is a pervasive, unconscious conspiracy in our country in which most of us participate, to discourage and suppress genuine leadership. A widespread, unspoken fear of the potentially negative consequences of creative leadership blankets our thoughts and actions. It prevents the most talented among us from speaking boldly or expressing ourselves as leaders. This conspiracy is all-encompassing, lulling us into conformity, complacency, cynicism, and inaction. As a nation—as organizations and as individuals—we fear taking risks. We do not expect ourselves or others to stand up and be counted, and we become frightened when they do. In a recent book, *The End of Management and the Rise of*

Organizational Democracy, coauthored with Kenneth Cloke, Joan argued that we have reached the end of an era in which bureaucracy, hierarchy, and autocracy thrive. Democracy requires leaders with integrity, authenticity, and the courage to stand for humane values. As bureaucracies defend themselves for survival, true leadership is seen as a threat to authoritarian rule and is shunned, attacked, and rejected.

We purposefully sound the alarm in these pages about the leadership *crisis* in our society because it is our hope that by raising this issue we will stir *you* to become aware of and take responsibility for our collective leadership challenge. Once we become aware of the barriers we face in expressing ourselves as leaders, we can transform ourselves into responsible, effective leaders who can break this unconscious conspiracy and demonstrate the courage to solve the problems of our time. For those of you who are willing to reshape yourselves as leaders, we suggest that you examine the public and private experiences in your own life when leadership was lacking and what happened as a result.

The first step in becoming a leader, then, is to recognize the culture for what it is—a breaker, not a maker; a trap, not a launching pad; an end, not a beginning—and declare your independence from and determination to change it.

Leaders from the Past—An Exercise

Our personal view of leadership is shaped by our experiences from the past. In part, we have all made decisions about leadership based on what we have learned from our families, communities, and schools, from direct encounters with leaders we have known, and from observations of distant heroes. We create unconscious patterns from these experiences that inform our present-day actions. To the extent that we are unaware of these patterns, or the contexts in which they arise, we are unconscious of the limits we have placed on our self-expression and leadership skills.

Who were your mentors? Who walked through your dreams? Who were the giants, larger than life, who inspired you to act? Who were the real people who made a difference in your life? In this exercise you will discover the hidden models you carry in your memories and in your heart. You will become aware of the women and men who shaped your expectations for yourself.

The answers to these questions and your comments on the following chart will reveal the experiences that shaped your personal view of leadership. You will gain a perspective on the leaders you knew and the decisions you made as a result of your perceptions. If you are working in a team, first complete the exercise as an individual, then compare and discuss your responses with your colleagues.

Leadership Models

1. Who were the leaders from your past whom you remember and revere? Whom do you consider a leader in your current life?

Questions to Consider

A. Name three people who walked through your dreams as leaders in the past.

. . . .

. . . .

. . . .

B. Name three leaders whom you respect and value who are currently in your life.

. . . .

. . . .

. . . .

2. What were the results of their leadership? How did their lives unfold? What happened to these leaders as a result of their expressions of leadership, in their personal lives, and on the larger stage of their work and accomplishments?

Questions to Consider

A. For each person from your past, indicate their successes and failures and your assessment of their achievements.

. . . .

. . . .

. . . .

. . . .

. . . .

. . . .

. . . .

B. As you view current leaders, indicate separately the obstacles they face in expressing their leadership abilities and the rewards they gain from being leaders.

. . . .

. . . .

. . . .

. . . .

. . . .

. . . .

. . . .

C. How would you assess these leaders in terms of the risks they took and the results they achieved? How would you sum up their lives?

. . . .

. . . .

. . . .

. . . .

. . . .

. . . .

. . . .

. . . .

3. What did you learn about leadership from your models? How did their personal characteristics, their views of their lives, and the actions they took have an impact on your vision of yourself?

Questions to Consider

A. As you live your life on a day-to-day basis, how could you use what you have learned from the leaders you have admired?

. . . .

. . . .

. . . .

. . . .

. . . .

. . . .

. . . .

. . . .

B. What positive and negative aspects of life and leadership did you learn from these men and women who shaped your views of leadership?

. . . .

. . . .

. . . .

. . . .
. . . .
. . . .
. . . .
. . . .

On the following chart, list six qualities, six attitudes, and six behaviors that characterize the leaders you remember and those you currently admire. Indicate what you learned from these leaders that has been valuable in your personal and professional life. In creating this chart, look for the qualities, attitudes, and behaviors that are common to several individuals so that you can identify what is most powerful and valuable. Finally, in the last column, summarize the leadership traits you have learned from these men and women who are your models. We have provided an example of these elements on the chart below.

Leadership Qualities, Attitudes, Behaviors, and Lessons Chart

QUALITIES	ATTITUDES	BEHAVIORS	LESSONS
personal integrity	constructive	outspoken	speak your mind
1. . . . .
2. . . . .
3. . . . .
4. . . . .
5. . . . .
6. . . . .

What do you learn from identifying the qualities, attitudes, behaviors, and lessons of the leaders in your life? Probe beneath the surface of the comments you made by answering the following questions.

Questions to Consider

A. What inspiring and positive lessons about life and leadership can you draw from the experiences of the leaders you have identified?

. . . .

. . . .

. . . .

. . . .

. . . .

. . . .

B. What cautions and negative conclusions do you notice as you analyze the lives of these women and men?

. . . .

. . . .

. . . .

. . . .

. . . .

. . . .

C. Given the qualities, attitudes, and behaviors of these leaders, what aspects of their lives had the greatest impact on your own life choices? Why were you particularly influenced by these qualities?

. . . .

. . . .

. . . .

. . . .

. . . .

. . . .

Working with a team or colleagues, create a chart that is a synthesis of the qualities, attitudes, behaviors, and lessons identified by yourself and the others with whom you are working. In creating this synthesis of all the ideas expressed, discuss the following:

Questions to Consider

    A. How did the insights about leadership differ for each member of your team?

    B. Were there disagreements among team members about the entries on the chart? If there were differences, discuss how each person viewed the qualities of leadership that influenced them.

    C. Notice that the same qualities and messages can be interpreted by some team members as positive and by others as negative. If that is so, discuss what informs these different points of view.

    D. If you are working in a team that is part of a larger group, have one member of your team present a summary of your synthesis to the larger group. Compare similarities and differences across groups.

    E. Notice any differences in leadership attributes that coincide with differences in position, role, organizational structure, length of time in the organization.

Myths About Leadership—An Exercise

One of the problems we face in recognizing leadership qualities and talents is that we are unaware of the subconscious myths about leadership that shape our beliefs. Every culture, whether societal or organizational, creates myths that in turn influence values, beliefs, and ways of thinking. These myths that operate in every culture tell us whom to acknowledge as our leaders.

In most cases, leadership myths do not support the emergence of unorthodox leaders. We have come to a place in our society where leadership myths have become quite restrictive and tend to hinder self-expression. Thus, a belief in these myths keeps us from taking risks. In order to assist you in becoming more aware of the influence of these myths on your thoughts and behaviors, we have described several below. As you read them, try to imagine times when you heard or experienced this myth.

In the space provided below describe a time when you thought the myth was true or when people you knew believed the myth and operated as if it were true.

Leadership Myths

1. Leadership Is a Rare Skill

Nothing could be further from the truth. While *great* leaders may be as rare as great runners, great actors, or great painters, everyone has leadership potential. There are millions of leadership roles being exercised throughout the world. People may be leaders in one organization and have quite ordinary roles in another. What distinguishes them is that they seize the moment and rise to the challenge.

. . . .

. . . .

. . . .

. . . .

. . . .

. . . .

. . . .

. . . .

2. Leaders Are Born, Not Made

Biographies of great leaders sometimes read as if they entered the world with an extraordinary genetic endowment, as if their future leadership role was pre-ordained. Do not believe it. The truth is that major capacities and competencies of leadership can be learned—if the desire to learn them exists.

This is not to suggest that it is easy to learn to be a leader. There is no simple formula, no rigorous science, no cookbook that produces, inexorably, successful leadership. Instead it is a deeply human process, full of trial and error, victories and defeats, timing and happenstance, intuition and insight.

. . . .

. . . .

. . . .

. . . .

. . . .

. . . .

. . . .

. . . .

. . . .

3. Leaders Are Charismatic

Some are, but most are not. Leaders, for the most part, are "all too human." They are short and tall, articulate and inarticulate, dress for success and dress for failure, and there is nothing in terms of appearance, personality, or style that sets them apart from their followers. Our guess is that charisma is rather the result of effective leadership, and those who master it are granted respect, even awe, by their followers, thus increasing the attraction between them.

. . . .

. . . .

. . . .

. . . .

. . . .

. . . .

. . . .

4. Leadership Exists Only at the Top of an Organization

We reinforce this myth by looking to the executives of large organizations for examples of leaders, but it is obviously false. In fact, the larger the organization, the more leadership roles it is likely to offer. General Motors has thousands of leadership roles available to employees, as does the United Auto Workers, its counterpart labor union.

. . . .

. . . .

. . . .

. . . .

. . . .

. . . .

. . . .

5. The Leader Controls, Directs, Prods, and Manipulates Others

This is perhaps the most damaging myth of all. Leadership is not so much the exercise of power *over* as the exercise of genuine empowerment *of* others. Leaders lead by pulling rather than by pushing; by creating achievable expectations and rewarding progress; by enabling people to use their own initiative.

. . . .

. . . .

. . . .

. . . .

. . . .

. . . .

. . . .

6. Other Myths

Can you think of other myths, misconceptions, and beliefs about leadership? Please add them to this list and share them with colleagues. If you are working in a team, create a list of the myths that are common to your organization.

. . . .

. . . .

. . . .

. . . .

. . . .

. . . .

. . . .

. . . .

. . . .

Questions to Consider

Who told you this myth was true?

Who lives their life by believing in this myth?

As you review each myth, who is the person whose life suggests that it is true?

With these myths revealed, we can now reflect on the implications that they have for our view of ourselves as leaders. Whether you reviewed these myths solo or as part of a team, the following questions will enable you to take them apart and analyze how they have an impact on you and the organization in which you work.

Questions to Consider

A. If you were able to identify individuals or incidents that exemplified a myth, state why the myth seemed to be true. What purpose did it serve? What was required from everyone else to reinforce the myth and perpetuate it?

. . . .

. . . .

. . . .

. . . .

. . . .

. . . .

. . . .

. . . .

B. What are the leadership myths in your organization? How does your organization propagate its leadership myths?

. . . .

. . . .

. . . .

. . . .

. . . .

. . . .

. . . .

. . . .

C. How do the leadership myths in your life influence your behavior and your self-assessment? What price have you paid as a result?

. . . .

. . . .

. . . .

. . . .

. . . .

. . . .

. . . .

. . . .

D. How do your position, role, and responsibilities in the organization shape your myths about leadership?

. . . .

. . . .

. . . .

. . . .

. . . .

. . . .

. . . .

. . . .

The Leadership Gap—An Exercise

Every day we encounter situations, circumstances, or seemingly impossible problems that might be ameliorated or solved by the exercise of leadership.

Often we are unaware that leadership is needed. Unseeing, we do not take action ourselves or empower others to fill the void. Our belief in the myths we have mentioned blinds us to our hidden potential for responding to the need for leaders. In an almost unconscious state, we do not recognize that we can be leaders and that we can make a difference. Instead, we may feel unsettled. We may have a nagging feeling that something is unexpressed. We may experience an uncomfortableness, a "dis-ease" with the flow of events and results that seems inevitable.

In the next exercise we seek to increase your awareness of the times and places when your leadership might have made a difference, that is, when it could have had an impact on the events in your life. By noticing when your leadership was required, where it was missing, and how this leadership gap occurred, you can begin to respond with thoughts and actions that might change your world and the lives of others.

We begin by asking you to focus your attention on the need for leadership in your larger community. To remind yourself of scenarios that could benefit from your leadership, review local and national newspapers, magazines, and other publications to identify problems and situations that are at an impasse and do not seem to have a resolution. We have provided examples to stimulate your thinking.

Questions to Consider

A. Create a list of situations that seem to be in turmoil or at an impasse and that might be forwarded or resolved by the intervention of a leader. Look for at least five situations.

1. *Conflict over use of public parks by people who are homeless.*

2. . . . .

3. . . . .

4. . . . .

5. . . . .

6. . . . .

7. . . . .

8. . . . .

9. . . . .

10. . . . .

11. . . . .

12. . . . .

13. . . . .

14. . . . .

15. . . . .

16. . . . .

17. . . . .

18. . . . .

19. . . . .

20. . . . .

B. Create a scenario for each situation that describes how it might be improved by your intervention as a leader.

1. *A leader is needed who can listen to both sides and design a problem-solving session in which both sides come together and mediate a solution.*

2. . . . .

3. . . . .

4. . . . .

5. . . . .

6. . . . .

7. . . . .

8. . . . .

C. What could you do to bring both sides together?
I can call the leaders of each faction and privately invite them to share their concerns with me and to come to a meeting to make their ideas known.

1. . . . .

2. . . . .

3. . . . .

4. . . . .

5. . . . .

6. . . . .

7. . . . .

8. . . . .

9. . . . .

10. . . . .

11. . . . .

12. . . . .

13. . . . .

14. . . . .

D. What keeps you from taking the action you know is needed to solve the problem? What leadership myths obstruct your view? What supports you in demonstrating leadership in this situation?

I have a fear of rejection and a feeling that I am at the bottom of the hierarchy with no power. I am blocked by the myth that leadership exists only at the top. I am also supported by friends who look to me for solutions and appreciate my interventions.

. . . .

. . . .

. . . .

. . . .

. . . .

. . . .

. . . .

E. What could you do to solve the problem? How would you demonstrate your leadership ability?

I would ask each side to meet with me. I would begin by listening to their points of view. I would then ask them to meet together and try to create a common vision to solve the problem. I would then work with them to come up with a solution that meets both sets of needs and supports their common vision.

. . . .

. . . .

. . . .

. . . .

. . . .

. . . .

. . . .

F. In a team, or with a partner, discuss one problem that you or a member of the team has identified. Assume you are consultants to a leader who must grapple with the situation. Come to consensus on the advice you want to give him and describe the advice below. In giving your advice, pay attention to ethical considerations and the personal agendas and skills of the leader. As you work on a real problem and its need for leadership, you may find your own solutions to seemingly intractable situations. As you find these hidden resources within yourself or in your team, acknowledge your successes and create a foundation for further growth and development.

. . . .

. . . .

. . . .

. . . .

. . . .

. . . .

. . . .

. . . .

. . . .

Leaders in Our Families—An Exercise

Many of us can make the charge that the novelist, Franz Kafka, so eloquently articulates in his *Diaries*:

> When I think about it, I must say that my education has done me great harm in some respects. This reproach applies to a multitude of people—that is to say, my parents, several relatives, individuals, visitors to my house, various writers, a crowd of teachers—a school inspector, slowly walking passers-by; in short, this reproach twists through society like a dagger. . . . I can prove any time that my education tried to make another person out of me than the one I became.

For the most part, our schools and families have failed to create a nurturing and supportive context for our development as leaders. As long as this context remains invisible to us, we cannot shift our thinking or our behavior to fill the leadership gap. Before we can learn to lead, we have to reexamine the context that builds or limits the full expression of our leadership. Indeed, anyone who does not master this context will be mastered by it. In this exercise we analyze the context that was created in our families.

We begin by focusing on our families of origin, the ones in which we grew up. They were the most powerful learning environments we ever experienced. It is in our families that we first develop a sense of our identity, our values, our aspirations, and our expectations for leadership. Yet it is in our families that we have the least examined and most determining experiences. Because family life is so powerful in influencing our views of leadership, and because we often maintain an unconscious barrier to recognizing its impact, it is difficult to make choices about the lessons we learned and the messages we received.

We propose that the place to begin is with discussions with your own immediate family members. If you are fortunate enough to have members of an older generation still living, you can start with them. If not, talk to siblings, cousins, and other members of your family of origin. If you are the sole member of your family, plumb your own memories. Try to discover answers to the following questions:

Questions to Consider

A. Who were considered leaders in your family? Who were heroes and heroines? What traits did they have? Make a list and notice who is included and who is excluded. Ask several family members the same questions and compare their responses. Who showed up on all the lists? Who are the people on your list who did not appear on the lists of others?

. . . .

. . . .

. . . .

. . . .

. . . .

. . . .

. . . .

. . . .

B. How did your family view leadership? Was it something far off in the distance that only "great men" exhibited? Were there leaders of both genders in your family, right in your own house? How was leadership defined differently for each gender or age group?

. . . .

. . . .

. . . .

. . . .

. . . .

. . . .

. . . .

. . . .

C. Were leaders identified with a particular role, a particular place in the sibling hierarchy, a special branch of the family, a particular gender, culture or race?

. . . .

. . . .

. . . .

. . . .

. . . .

73

. . . .

. . . .

. . . .

D. What were the signals sent to you about being a leader? Who sent them, and how were they delivered? Was the communication subtle or direct? How did you respond? Did you rebel or did you conform?

. . . .

. . . .

. . . .

. . . .

. . . .

. . . .

. . . .

E. How were you encouraged or discouraged to exercise your leadership skills? What decision about yourself did you make on the basis of these expectations?

. . . .

. . . .

. . . .

. . . .

. . . .

. . . .

. . . .

If you are able to work on this exercise in a team, compare notes and exchange anecdotes. Notice the variety of responses from different families. As a team, collect common themes, insights, and conclusions. What are the different attitudes toward leadership expressed in different families? How did gender, culture, race, ethnicity, immigration, and social class influence leadership patterns? As you exchange your observations, your family's contribution to your view of leadership may become clearer.

You now have an opportunity to create a family tree that diagrams the history of leadership for generations past in your own family. There are many approaches to genealogical research and family trees. We have designed the leadership family tree included here for you to use in diagramming your family's history in relation to leadership. In this exercise, we invite you to use the diagram and fill in the information for your ancestors, going back as many generations as you can. By creating your family tree, notice the legacies, models, and messages that have been passed down to you through the generations. Notice the participation in leadership roles by your family members, the ones they assumed and those they did not. Knowledge of our family history allows each of us to become more conscious of the choices available to us. Susan Griffin, in her extraordinary book *A Chorus of Stones*, writes about the importance of embracing family history:

> I am beginning to believe that we know everything, that all history, including the history of each family, is part of us, such that, when we hear any secret revealed, a secret about a grandfather, or an uncle, . . . our lives are made suddenly clearer to us, as the unnatural heaviness of unspoken truth is dispersed. For perhaps we are like stones; our own history and the history of the world embedded in us, we hold a sorrow deep within and cannot weep until that history is sung.

The leadership roles you enter on your chart may focus on different aspects of your early life: church, synagogue, family, school, community, work, and the larger world. Include any expression of leadership that you can remember or discover in your family history. You may also want to ask your spouse or partner to complete a similar chart and compare it with yours. Notice the patterns you each have inherited. Observe how you carry these patterns into your current family and work environment. Do you notice any parallels? When you have completed the chart, show it to a family member and discuss your observations. It is through these conversations that our "history is sung," as Susan Griffin describes it, and that we are released from the hold of unconscious patterns from the past.

In each box in the chart, list the name of the person and the leadership role they played. You may want to use one color for you and your direct ancestors, and another color for members of your extended family.

Leaders in Our Organizations—An Exercise

We carry our family patterns with us to work. These are reshaped, revised, and revisited as we interact with the values, culture, and expectations of the organizations that house us in our adult lives. We learn about leadership from our colleagues in these organizations, and we also learn from the structures and systems of the organization itself.

Take a dispassionate look at your place of work, the environment in which you spend the majority of your waking hours. How are leaders viewed, rewarded, and developed? How are they discouraged or punished? What has been the impact of their implicit and explicit messages on your vision of yourself and your role as a leader?

Complete the following chart by indicating the ways your work environment supports the expression of leadership on an ongoing basis and the ways it discourages the development of new leadership. Please note, as you engage in this analysis, that organizations express their support or discouragement of leadership through explicit rewards, promotions, and acknowledgment. Other, more subtle means of signaling attitudes toward leadership—such as training programs, social events, communication systems, and staff structures—also have an impact. In completing this exercise you will want to observe the hidden as well as the explicit signals that are sent in support or suppression of leadership. Also note how traditional as well as new forms of leadership are selected or encouraged.

Leadership Family Tree

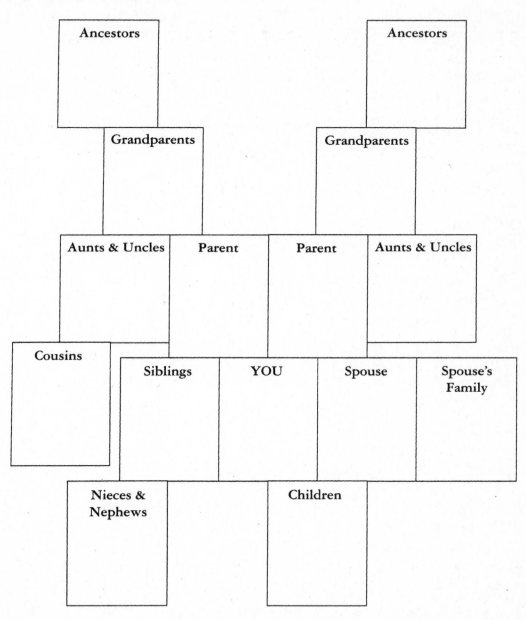

Organizational Leadership Chart

Ways My Organization Supports
Expressions of Leadership

Ways My Organization Obstructs
Expressions of Leadership

. . . .
. . . .
. . . .
. . . .
. . . .
. . . .
. . . .

If you have completed this chart in analyzing your work environment by your-self, show your chart to a colleague or friend who knows your work situation and ask for feedback on your perceptions. If you are working in a team, have each individual complete the chart.

Activities to Consider

A. Compare charts with team members and discuss their differences and similarities.

B. Discuss specific examples of situations that have supported or obstructed leadership.

C. First, have your team come to consensus on the supports and obstacles to leadership, then complete a team chart that shows this consensus.

D. Next, if you are part of a larger group, present your team chart to other teams. Discuss the common factors and explain the underlying dynamics that produced them.

As you examine your work environment, take a look at how it has influenced the choices you have made. What has been its impact on your behavior? How has it shaped your expression of yourself? Who are the colleagues you respect and emulate? When have you stood up to be counted? When have you held back from playing a leadership role?

Questions to Consider

Now we will take a look at how your legacy from the past has influenced your ability to be a leader. If you are working alone, think of two scenarios: one in which you played a leadership role at work, and one in which you avoided being a leader. For each scenario consider these questions:

A. The patterns I've discovered from my family history that block or support me as a leader are:

. . . .

. . . .

. . . .

. . . .

B. The messages I have received from my work environment that have encouraged or discouraged me as a leader are:

. . . .

. . . .

. . . .

. . . .

C. The comfort or discomfort I feel in playing the role of leader is:

. . . .

. . . .

. . . .

. . . .

. . . .

D. The rewards or punishments I have received for my past leadership behaviors were:

. . . .

. . . .

. . . .

. . . .

. . . .

E. The decisions I made as a result of my experiences or the responses of others are:

. . . .

. . . .

. . . .

. . . .

. . . .

After you have answered these questions, you may want to share your responses with your colleagues and compare them with the experiences of other people. In this chapter we have worked to understand the leadership crisis in society and the implications it has for your life. In reflecting on the challenges before you, you may want to decide to take new actions, express a new commitment to making a difference, and revise your goals as a leader. If you notice any changes you would like to make in your own leadership behaviors, we encourage you to act on your insights and your instincts. Leaders often receive no mandate for action other than the signals they receive from their inner voice telling them it is now time to take a stand or make a move. To assist you in these important contemplations, the next chapter will enable you to understand yourself more deeply and consider the role self-knowledge plays in becoming a leader.

4 Knowing Yourself

I have often thought that the best way to define a man's character would be to seek out the particular mental or moral attitude in which, when it came upon him, he felt himself most deeply and intensively active and alive. At such moments, there is a voice inside which speaks and says, "This is the real me."

William James, *The Letters of William James*

L EADERS KNOW THEMSELVES; THEY KNOW WHAT THEY CAN DO WELL. Part of their secret is that they have positive self-regard, they know their talents, build on their strengths, and are able to discern how they can contribute to their organizations, their communities, and the quality of life of those around them.

The intense and complicated journey you have begun here to develop yourself as a leader and achieve a positive sense of yourself begins with a detailed knowledge of your limitations and abilities. Once you understand what it takes for you to learn about yourself, you can solicit and integrate feedback from others. If you continually keep yourself open to new experiences and information, listen to your inner voice, and observe your actions with a critical eye, this process will succeed.

Self-reflection is a critical step in becoming a leader. It starts when you reflect on your experiences, including both successes and failures. Self-reflective moments may come with a lightning bolt of instant insight, or they may slowly evolve through writing in a journal, going on a contemplative retreat, or requesting a coaching from a trusted colleague. In this process you gain clarity about who you are and how you express the multifaceted aspects of yourself. You listen for the voice that spoke to William James, saying, "This is the real me."

A second source of information for knowing yourself may come from asking the people with whom you work how they have experienced your behavior. Receiving "reflective feedback" from friends, colleagues, spouses, and significant others allows you to be true to yourself in relation to their perceptions. With this input, you can enrich your self-knowledge.

Being *continually* open to learning provides you with a third source of self-knowledge. Remaining open to new ideas and ways of learning might include being truthful with yourself and others, being willing to reevaluate prior beliefs in the face of new information, and continuing to be clear about your vision, values, goals, and priorities.

A fourth way of knowing yourself is by closely tracking the connection between what you believe and what you do and say. This means continually searching for ways of maintaining and expanding your integrity. It means being of one piece internally and externally, so that you express yourself fully, completely, and consistently. Max DePree, founder and former CEO of the Herman Miller Company, said it best in the moving prologue to his book *Leadership Jazz:*

> Esther, my wife, and I have a granddaughter named Zoe, the Greek word for "life." She was born prematurely and weighed one pound, seven ounces, so small that my wedding ring could slide up her arm to her shoulder. The neonatologist who first examined her told us that she had a 5 to 10 percent chance of living three days.
>
> To complicate matters, Zoe's biological father had jumped ship the month before Zoe was born. Realizing this, a wise and caring nurse named Ruth gave me my instructions. "For the next several months, at least, you're the surrogate father. I want you to come to the hospital every day to visit Zoe, and when you come, I would like you to rub her body and her legs and arms with the tip of your finger. While you're caressing her, you should tell her over

and over how much you love her, because she has to be able to connect your voice with your touch."

Ruth was doing exactly the right thing on Zoe's behalf (and of course, on my behalf as well), and without realizing it she was giving me one of the best possible descriptions of the work of a leader. At the core of becoming a leader is the need always to connect one's voice and one's touch.

Leaders are able to hear their our own internal voice and recognize the power of using it to touch others. If you have a clear awareness of who you are and how you can express it to others, you can develop the constancy that Max DePree was able to show in helping Zoe strengthen her life force.

Shifting the Leadership Paradigm

"Paradigm" has become a trendy word in social science literature in recent years. The popularity of the concept probably stems from the realization that our current way of thinking, seeing the world, and interpreting data is not effective in producing the results we hope to achieve. We not only need new ideas; we need new *ways* of creating and implementing them. In transforming yourself as a leader, you will recognize the paradigm through which you view life, and shift this paradigm in order to see yourself and your capacity for leadership in a new way.

A paradigm is a framework, a construct, a contextual perspective through which we view experience. A shift in a widely held paradigm has far-reaching consequences. Fifteenth-century Europe transformed its thinking not only about the earth's placement in the universe as a result of Galileo's discovery that it circled the sun but also changed views widely held about the role of the father as the center of family life and the king as the sole leader of society. From seeing the earth as the center of the universe to consideration of this planet as one of many power centers caused a major shift in the prevalent paradigm. As a result, personal, social, and political thought opened to a more complex, nuanced recognition of multiple sources of power, authority, and knowledge.

Paradigms that have shifted in our lifetime include the increased leadership role and acceptance of women in government, religion, and business; the view of Russia as an ally and partner to the United States; and the belief that all Americans are entitled to civil rights and voting privileges regardless of race. In our view, a new leadership paradigm is needed to transform the economic, social, and political conditions that are currently in crisis. We are calling for changes that go beyond a critical stance or different rhetoric. With a shift in leadership paradigms comes a new orientation toward society; new roles and ways of behaving; and new values, morals, and commitments that reorient us to what it means to be human.

Before this shift in our leadership paradigm takes place, we need to be aware of the old conceptual frameworks through which we have seen the world. We need to know them for what they are and recognize their impact on our global perceptions. To make clearer the leadership paradigms that have led us to the difficulties we now face, please review the following three elements of the old paradigm that are presented below. As you increase your awareness of these ways of seeing leadership, you can begin to understand how they have shaped your hesitations and biases about becoming a leader.

1. *Leaders Are Great Men Who Are More Qualified to Lead Than I Am*

This is the silver-spoon theory of leadership. According to this ancient paradigm, leaders already have the correct lineage and were endowed from birth with the looks, personalities, and access to wealth, power, and authority that make them qualified to lead. In this paradigm, organizational behavior is characterized by apathy, cynicism, and mindless obedience.

2. *Good Management Makes Successful Organizations*

The nineteenth-century managerial model of organizations still pervades our institutions. In this paradigm, we assume that if we have efficient top-down managers and produce short-term results, we will be successful. In this paradigm, organizational behavior is characterized by hierarchical, bureaucratic, and autocratic forms of management that thrive in the absence of leadership.

3. *Failure Is to Be Avoided at All Costs*

Most of us have been raised to believe that leaders never fail. This belief tells us that we cannot be leaders because we make mistakes, and that if leaders do make mistakes, their failures should be hidden, swept under the rug, denied, and passed on by blaming others. In this paradigm, organizational behavior is characterized by risk avoidance and fear.

How many times have you viewed your work experience through these ideas? In this chapter, you have an opportunity to create a new paradigm of leadership, one that will validate your experience and support you in "doing the right thing" rather than only focusing on "doing things right." It will encourage you to take risks and learn from the failures you face along the way.

To shift your thinking and behavior from one paradigm to another, we suggest that you first become aware of the pervasiveness of your old way of thinking. Next, we ask you to define a new paradigm of leadership. Finally, we ask you to take action based on the assumptions embedded in your new way of thinking. Good leaders don't simply observe, they *act*, *invent* as they go along, *learn* from their mistakes, and *adapt* to changing conditions. This ability of leaders to act, invent, learn, and adapt challenges another paradigm: that leaders have everything figured out in advance. Instead, leaders move according to the prompts of their internal compasses, taking risks along the way, stumbling, inventing, learning, and adapting according to changing circumstances. But here is the difference: They don't learn simply because life forces lessons upon them; they are *proactive* learners. In other words, they make accidents, chaos, and indeterminacy work for them. Engaging a new paradigm for leadership that is more viable in today's world requires that you learn how to lead in just this way. This new way of thinking about leadership is based on a new paradigm that includes these ideas: Everyone can create themselves as a leader in their own life through a process of self-transformation; leaders rather than managers need to be at the helm of successful organizations; and failure is a valuable source of learning, improvement, and growth.

⚓ Leaders Learn How to Learn—An Exercise

We begin creating this new paradigm of leadership by exploring our capacity to learn something new. As adults, we rarely have the opportunity to place ourselves in the role of learner. Some of us may have had the experience of the role of student by going back to school to earn a degree, or by participating in a special seminar or institute. We may have attended an in-service or on-the-job educational program in our company or organization. But, too often, the learning environment we encounter is low-risk and protected. In these cases, we can passively skate through meeting someone else's course requirements without ever having to confront our basic assumptions.

The learning process we are advocating here provides a vastly different quality of inquiry that includes active, risky, self-conscious, and committed learning. This approach to learning enables you to experience the transformation as a leader in today's complex and crisis-rich environment. This learning approach involves much more than absorbing a body of knowledge or mastering a discipline. It calls for seeing the world simultaneously as it is and as it might be, understanding the distinction between the two, and acting to bridge the gap.

Ideally, if you want to understand more about *how* you learn, you might consider engaging in an activity you have avoided or believed you could never perform. For example, you might decide to participate for the first time in an Outward Bound Program, or learn skiing, whitewater rafting, mountain climbing, skydiving, or bungee-jumping. These dramatic physical challenges will teach you everything you need to know about your learning style and confront you with the assumptions you hold about yourself. As you do, you may turn your world upside down. Learning to become a leader sometimes takes just that.

If you have the opportunity to choose a physically demanding learning challenge, we encourage you to take the risk. However, you do not need to leap giant buildings in a single bound in order to learn about how you learn. Volunteer to give a speech, run a meeting, act in a local theater company, learn to play the piano, spend time getting to know people with whom you disagree, drive to an unknown community, or spend a day alone in unfamiliar territory. If your life permits, test yourself with a mode of behavior that is very different from the one to which you've grown accustomed. It will give you the insights you need to learn about your learning style.

As you take on a new and challenging experience, listen to your inner voice, observe your feelings, reactions, and internal dialogue. When it is over, spend time reflecting on what happened. Take time to think about what you did, how it felt, and how you did it. If you cannot engage in a new experience, remember when you learned something new and experienced a departure from your normal routine. Reflect either on your experience from the past or on one you initiated for this exercise. And remember, as French novelist Marcel Proust wrote, "The real voyage of discovery consists not in seeking new landscapes, but in having new eyes."

Questions to Consider

A. Begin by describing in detail the challenge, the new experience, and the risk you selected as the focus for reflection on your learning style.

. . . .

. . . .

. . . .

. . . .

. . . .

. . . .

. . . .

. . . .

. . . .

. . . .

B. What were your fears before you began the experience? How did those fears change and evolve before, during, and after the experience? What did you learn in the process about your fears?

. . . .

. . . .

. . . .

. . . .

. . . .

. . . .

. . . .

. . . .

. . . .

. . . .

C. What have others told you about yourself in the past that either supported or undermined your confidence when taking the risk to learn something new?

. . . .

. . . .

. . . .

. . . .

. . . .

. . . .

. . . .

. . . .

. . . .

D. What seemed to be the greatest risk before you started? How did your assessment of the risks involved change as the experience progressed?

. . . .
. . . .
. . . .
. . . .
. . . .
. . . .
. . . .
. . . .
. . . .
. . . .

E. What external people, circumstances, actions, and events most supported your learning? Which ones blocked your development of new skills, insights, or levels of achievement?

. . . .
. . . .
. . . .
. . . .
. . . .
. . . .
. . . .
. . . .
. . . .
. . . .

89

F. What was it about your thinking and behavior that contributed most to your learning? What aspects blocked your learning?

. . . .

. . . .

. . . .

. . . .

. . . .

. . . .

. . . .

. . . .

. . . .

. . . .

G. At what point did you know you were successful? How did you know you were successful? What evidence do you have of success?

. . . .

. . . .

. . . .

. . . .

. . . .

. . . .

. . . .

. . . .

. . . .

. . . .

H. What were the high points, the joys, and the payoffs of the risks you took?

. . . .

. . . .

. . . .

. . . .

. . . .

. . . .

. . . .

. . . .

. . . .

. . . .

I. How did your image of yourself and your understanding of who you are change as a result of your experience?

. . . .

. . . .

. . . .

. . . .

. . . .

. . . .

. . . .

. . . .

. . . .

. . . .

J. What new experiences grew out of this one? How did you change your idea of yourself as a leader because of what you learned?

. . . .

. . . .

. . . .

. . . .

. . . .

. . . .

. . . .

. . . .

. . . .

. . . .

The risks of learning to become a leader are similar to the risks involved in any new challenge. Your answers to the questions above will give you information about your approach to learning from new experiences. This information is important in understanding your learning capacity and style as a leader. From this exercise you can see the behaviors, the thinking, and the support it will take to enable you to overcome your fears and break new ground as a leader.

Learning Modes—An Exercise

Each of us has our own way of learning something new. How many times have you argued with loving companions when they told you how to go about a new project you planned in a way that was completely different than the one they suggested? Gib Akin, associate professor at the McIntire School of Commerce, University of Virginia, studied the learning experiences of sixty leaders. Writing for *Organizational Dynamics*, Akin found that these leaders' descriptions were surprisingly congruous. He found that they routinely reported that the learning experience was personally transformative. Akin found the leaders in his study learned in a variety of ways, including:

- **Emulation**, in which one emulates either someone one knows or a historical or public figure;
- **Role taking**, in which one has a conception of what one should do and does it;
- **Practical accomplishment**, in which one sees a problem as an opportunity and learns through the experience of dealing with it;
- **Validation**, in which one tests concepts by applying them and learns after the fact;
- **Anticipation**, in which one develops a concept and then applies it, learning before acting;
- **Personal growth**, in which one is less concerned with specific skills than with self-understanding and the transformation of values and attitudes;
- **Scientific learning**, in which one observes and conceptualizes on the basis of one's observations, then experiments to gather new data, with a primary focus on finding the truth.

In our view, each of the modes of learning that Akin describes is valid under different circumstances, to solve various problems, to conform to different thinking styles, and to meet a variety of learning needs. Each mode has positive and negative qualities that determine when they are appropriate for use. Successful leaders are not locked into a single mode of learning. For example, in some circumstances it may be best to figure out a solution yourself through a practical accomplishment mode and learn from the results you have produced. Yet if you have a teacher who has "been there and done that," it may be more appropriate to emulate her and sort out the consequences of her approach after you have tried her way of doing things.

By using the following chart, identify a situation in which you have applied each mode of learning, and then reflect on the positive and negative aspects that each mode had for you.

Modes of Learning Chart

Mode	*Situation*	*Positive Aspect*	*Negative Aspect*
Emulation			
Role Taking			
Practical Accomplishment			
Validation			
Anticipation			
Personal Growth			
Scientific Learning			

As you learn to become a better leader, review this chart and choose a different *way* of learning a new skill. Do you want to find a mentor to emulate? Is it best for you to jump in feet first and learn through practical accomplishment? Would you rather focus on self-understanding or on practical skills to transform yourself? Choose the mode or modes that best serve both your style and what you want to learn.

A Learning Style Presentation—An Exercise

Now that you have reflected on how you might learn something new, gained an understanding of what it will take for you to learn to be a leader, and reviewed your choices of different modes of learning, you may consolidate this knowledge. The following framework will give you an opportunity to spell out how you want to learn and how you will overcome the barriers to developing new skills. If you are working alone, write the description of yourself as if you were presenting it to others. If you have colleagues with whom you are sharing your learning process, introduce yourself by communicating what you know about your learning style. Use this as an opportunity to elicit feedback from the group. If you are working alone, reflect on your responses and determine what you need to do to become a more effective learner.

Present Your Learning Style

If you are working with others, start by saying, "I'd like to tell you about how I approach a risky learning situation. I'd also like to tell you about the learning modes that I find most useful for me. Based on your knowledge of my learning style, please give me your feedback about how I can become a better learner."

A recent important learning experience I have had was when I

. . . .

. . . .

What I learned from that experience was

. . . .

. . . .

I enjoy learning new things when I feel

. . . .

. . . .

The modes I like to use to learn something new are

. . . .

. . . .

In order to feel safe enough to try something new that may be threatening I need

. . . .

. . . .

I have the most difficulty learning something new when

. . . .

. . . .

I take the most pride and joy from learning when I have

. . . .

. . . .

The next time I am in a new learning situation I would like your support by

. . . .

. . . .

The next challenge I would like to face with your support is

. . . .

. . . .

The leaders Akin interviewed cited two basic motivations for their learning. They had a hunger to learn when they were not fulfilling their potential or when they were not expressing themselves fully. They knew that learning was the way toward self-expression. They saw learning as something intimately connected with self. No one taught them this idea in school. They had to teach it to themselves. Somehow they had reached a point in life where they knew they had to learn new things. For these leaders, the choice was to either take the risk to learn something new, or admit they had settled for less than they were capable of achieving. If you agree, as these leaders did, that risky learning is the only alternative worth taking, the next step is to become responsible for completing your education yourself.

Failure—The Springboard of Hope

Perhaps the most unusual and determining quality of how leaders learn is how they respond to failure. They simply don't think about it. One of them said during our interviews that "a mistake is just another way of doing things." Another said, "If I have an art form of leadership, it is to make as many mistakes as quickly as I can in order to learn." Like Karl Wallenda, the great tightrope aerialist—whose life was at stake each time he walked the tightrope—leaders put all their energies into focusing on the task at hand and being successful in responding to the risks they take. Wallenda believed, like many leaders, that "being on the tightrope is living; everything else is waiting."

Shortly after Wallenda fell to his death in 1978 traversing a high wire 75 feet above downtown San Juan, Puerto Rico, his wife, also an aerialist, discussed that fateful San Juan walk, which was "perhaps his most dangerous." She recalled: "All Karl thought about for three straight months prior to that walk was *falling*. It was the first time he'd ever thought about that, and it seemed to me that he put all his energies into *not falling* rather than walking the tightrope." In fact, Wallenda was so focused on not falling that at the beginning of his fall he held on to his balance stick too long and did not grab the high wire to stop his fall to prevent his death.

Every leader lives with his own version of the tightrope walk. From what we know about successful leaders, it is clear that when Wallenda poured his energies into *not falling* rather than walking the tightrope, he became virtually destined to fall. An example of the "Wallenda factor" appears in our interview with Fletcher Byrom, former president of the Koppers Company, a diversified engineering, construction, and chemicals company. When asked about the "hardest decision he ever had to make," he responded this way:

> I don't know what a hard decision is. I may be a strange animal but I don't worry. Whenever I make a decision, I start out recognizing there's a strong likelihood I'm going to be wrong. All I can do is the best I can. To worry puts obstacles in the way of clear thinking.

Or consider Ray Meyer—among the winningest coaches in college basketball history, who led DePaul University to forty-two consecutive winning seasons. When his team dropped its first game after twenty-nine straight home-court victories, his response was: "Great! Now we can start concentrating on winning, *not* on not losing." Meyer's comment emphasizes the capacity to embrace positive goals, to pour one's energies into the task, to not look backward and dredge up excuses for past events.

For a lot of people, the word "failure" carries with it a finality, an absence of movement characteristic of a dead thing, to which the automatic human reaction is one of helpless discouragement. But for the successful leader, failure is a beginning, the springboard of hope.

John Cleese, in addition to his memorable comic career in movies and with the British comedy ensemble Monty Python, writes and produces organizational development films that combine humor and wisdom. In a piece for *Forbes* magazine several years ago, Cleese exhorted the heads of organizations to adopt a policy that announced "No More Mistakes and You're Through." He pointed out that creativity, innovation, and human progress is based on learning from failure. The scientific method, creativity in the arts, and individual human growth includes error and adjustment based on learning. Cleese observed:

> It's self-evident that if we can't take the risk of saying or doing something wrong, our creativity goes right out the window. . . . The essence of creativity is not the possession of some special talent, it is much more the ability to

play. . . . In organizations where mistakes are not allowed, you get two types of counterproductive behavior. First, since mistakes are "bad" if they're committed by the people at the top, people can pretend that no mistake has been made. So it doesn't get fixed. Second, if they're committed by people lower down in the organization, mistakes get concealed.

For an organization to truly encourage independent thinking, to produce the best decisions, and to implement the wisest policies, it must encourage both learning and the mistakes it inevitably engenders.

Patterns of Failure—An Exercise

Where did our attitudes and beliefs about mistakes, failures, and wrong turns begin? Observing a young child beginning to walk is a lesson in failure. The child falls hundreds of times before he gets the knack of standing on two feet and propelling forward or backward. He does not stop to feel wrong, guilty, or embarrassed. He is determined to walk. Each fall is only a necessary part of the learning process. Do you remember learning to ride a bicycle? You probably applied the same methodology. You probably did not stop to worry about your failures. You probably did not refuse to ride again after every skinned knee. You continued to weave and wobble and get back on the bike again and again until you mastered the bicycle and, at the same time, yourself.

As you have grown into adulthood, you have probably assumed a different attitude toward mistakes. If the view of failure that you have adopted as an adult is rigid and punishing, you will block your ability to take risks, stand up for what you know is true, and respond to situations that demand your leadership. Where did you learn this view of failure? How have these patterns been reinforced throughout your adult life?

The following exercise will give you an opportunity to return to your past and see the life-altering experiences that shaped your attitudes toward your own failures. You will need help from a spouse, partner, or small team of colleagues to carry it out. If you are working in a team, one person should volunteer to read the instructions aloud to the group as everyone else goes through the process. If you are with a partner, one person should read the instructions while the other person follows the internal journey. After your partner has helped you, give her an opportunity to go through the process herself. The purpose of this process is to help you discover the origins of your patterns regarding failure.

To begin, read the instructions to yourself. In this guided imaging process, please accept the insights you gain, the images you see, and the feelings you experience as being right and appropriate for you. *You cannot make mistakes in this exercise.* You may fall asleep or may not see any pictures or feel any sensations. You may see a color or hear a sound or gain insights into your patterns regarding failure. Whatever happens is fine. Just follow the instructions as they are read by your partner or group leader and accept whatever comes from your experience.

In the course of this process, you or others may experience strong feelings. Do not open your eyes or interrupt the exercise. Let the feelings be part of the process as you continue. Below are the phrases to be read and suggested pauses and acknowledgments to make the guided imaging process go smoothly.

Guided Imaging Instructions

Sit in a comfortable position with your back against a chair and your feet firmly on the floor. [Pause.] Good.

Uncross your legs and hands and rest them in a relaxed position on your lap. [Pause.] Good.

Gently let your eyes close. Easily take several deep breaths and slowly release them. [Pause.] With each breath let your eyes relax and let your body release any tension that is there. [Pause.] Good.

Notice any sounds or movements in the room and release your attention from these sounds and movements. [Pause.] Good.

Let any thoughts come into your consciousness, and then release these thoughts. [Pause.] Good.

Let any emotions come into your consciousness, and then release these emotions. [Pause.] Good.

Let any pictures from the past come into your consciousness, and then release these pictures. [Pause.] Good.

Now you are sitting comfortably in your chair. [Pause.] You have let go of any noises or movements in the room. [Pause.] You have released all your tensions, thoughts, emotions, and pictures from your past. [Pause.] Good.

Now focus your attention on your feet and legs. If there is any tension there, release it. [Pause.] Good.

Now focus your attention on your abdomen and lower body. If there is any tension there, release it. [Pause.] Good.

Now focus your attention on your chest, shoulders, and arms. If there is any tension there, release it. [Pause.] Good.

Now focus your attention on your neck, head, and face. If there is any tension there, release it. [Pause.] Good.

Now you are fully relaxed and open to whatever is there for you. [Pause.] Good.

Remember a time when you failed at something. [Pause.] Just let the memory come into your consciousness. Stay with the memory for a moment or two. [Slightly longer pause.] Notice who is with you. [Pause.] Notice how you felt.

Remember a time when someone with whom you were close was told they were a failure. [Pause.] Just let the memory come into your consciousness. [Pause.] Who told them they were a failure? Stay with the memory for a minute or two. [Pause.] Notice what they did that others thought was a failure. [Pause.] Notice how they felt. [Pause.] Notice how you felt. [Pause.] Good.

Remember a time when someone told you, directly or indirectly, that you were a failure. [Pause.] Just let the memory come into your consciousness. Stay with the memory for a minute or two. [Pause.] Notice who told you that you were a failure. [Pause.] Notice how you felt. [Pause.] Good.

Remember a time when you succeeded at something, or someone told you, directly or indirectly, that you were a success. [Pause.] Just let the memory come into your consciousness. Stay with the memory for a minute or two. [Pause.] Notice who is with you, and who told you that you were a success. [Pause.] Notice how you felt. [Pause.] Good.

Let any feelings you have associated with these incidents reveal themselves, and then release them. [Pause.] Good.

If you have anything you want to say to the person who told you that you were a failure, say it to them in your mind now. [Pause.] Good.

If you have anything you want to say to the person who told you that you were a success, say it to them in your mind now. [Pause.] Good.

If you have any feelings about any failure you have had to which you want to say goodbye, say goodbye now. [Pause.] Good.

Now let go of all the images you have had in your mind, and just relax. [Pause.] Good.

Remain in a relaxed, peaceful state. [Pause.] Just let any feelings, thoughts, or pictures come to the surface and release them.

Now begin to feel the back of the chair next to your body and the floor under your feet. [Pause.] Good.

Begin to return your attention to the room. [Pause.] Good.

Begin to hear the noises in the room. Notice the movements around you. [Pause.] Good.

As I count to five, return your attention to the room. One. [Pause.] Two. [Pause.] Three. [Pause.] Four. [Pause.] Five. [Pause.] Open your eyes, and say hello to someone here in the room. Thank you.

Now that you've completed the process, turn to your partner or someone next to you and share what you learned. You may have had a number of insights, images, and feelings that came to the surface during this exercise. It is now time to take a look at the origin of your views about failure and how they impact your current life.

Labeling an action or a person as a "failure" is an arbitrary decision that you or someone else made sometime in the past. You then attached meanings, associations, decisions, and feelings to the concept of failure. In the present, you can now transform your past associations, ideas, and decisions about failure into ones that can enable you to become a better leader. Rather than getting stuck, feeling depressed, denigrating yourself, or using the memory of failure as evidence of your low self-worth, consider an alternative: Failure is an opportunity to learn, to change course, and to discover new options for yourself.

Each of us makes many mistakes in the course of every day. Some we notice because we are sensitive to a particular mistake, or because someone has called attention to it. However, in shifting our paradigm about leadership, we have an opportunity to change our view of failure also. In this new way of thinking, we have a choice: We can consider each mistake a natural part of life from which we can learn and grow, or we can use failure as evidence that we are not a worthwhile person and give up even trying.

David Hare, the playwright, told a wonderful story about Joseph Papp, impresario and director of the New York Shakespeare Festival, at a memorial for Papp just after his death in November 1991:

> The greatest thing Joe ever did was when we did "The Knife." There was a party afterward and the reviews were read. The *Times* review was absolutely dismal. He read it out line by line and the whole room went completely silent. It meant that we had lost over a million dollars. At the end he said, "That is not what I call a good review." Then he turned to me and said, "What do you want to do in my theater next?"

In shifting to a new paradigm regarding failure, start by discussing with your partner or team the insights about yourself that you have identified as a result of analyzing your greatest failure.

In Chapter 3 we investigated the models and patterns of leadership that we had learned in our families. Now we can probe deeper into our family experiences to find the origin of our ideas about failure. As a first step in this exploration, you may want to reflect on the questions we have included below. Next, you may want to discuss your answers with family members and friends. As you do so, ask for their insights about your history and compare your memories regarding failure with the remembrances of others.

Questions to Consider

A. What were the main messages in your family of origin regarding failure? What messages were sent to you? What messages were sent to others? How were they communicated? How did you accept, reject, and selectively reinforce them?

. . . .

. . . .

. . . .

. . . .

. . . .

. . . .

. . . .

. . . .

B. How were you treated when you failed? How did you respond? What happened when you succeeded?

. . . .

. . . .

. . . .

. . . .

. . . .

. . . .

. . . .

. . . .

C. What decisions did you make about your own failure or that of others?

. . . .

. . . .

. . . .

. . . .

. . . .

. . . .

. . . .

. . . .

D. How have you perpetuated these early views of failure in your adult personal life or in your relationships?

. . . .

. . . .

. . . .

. . . .

. . . .

. . . .

. . . .

. . . .

E. How did you apply them to your work or professional life?

. . . .

. . . .

. . . .
. . . .
. . . .
. . . .
. . . .
. . . .

F. In what ways have you passed them on to your children or younger colleagues?

. . . .
. . . .
. . . .
. . . .
. . . .
. . . .
. . . .
. . . .

G. What impact have they had on your relationships with colleagues, superiors, and subordinates?

. . . .
. . . .
. . . .
. . . .
. . . .
. . . .
. . . .

H. Who told you that you were a failure or that you should be careful to never fail?

. . . .

. . . .

. . . .

. . . .

. . . .

. . . .

. . . .

I. Regarding the person who most imprinted your views of failure, what was it about that person's life that motivated him or her to give you these messages about failure?

. . . .

. . . .

. . . .

. . . .

. . . .

. . . .

. . . .

J. How was this person serving his or her own needs in telling you about your failure?

. . . .

. . . .

. . . .

. . . .

. . . .

. . . .

. . . .

. . . .

K. What did you do with the information this person gave you about failure?

. . . .

. . . .

. . . .

. . . .

. . . .

. . . .

. . . .

It may be difficult to answer these questions about the past and how family members who loved you and whom you loved created dysfunctional attitudes toward failing. We believe, however, that it is important to trace the roots of your belief system in order to see yourself realistically and to transform your ways of thinking.

As you understand your thinking and feelings about failure, you may begin to see an alternative to your old paradigm about leadership. It takes a conscious effort to start thinking about mistakes, problems, and failure in a new way. The next exercise may help you make this paradigmatic shift.

The Leadership Checklist—An Exercise

If we do not accept failure, we will not be able to support creative discovery or encourage risk-taking in organizations. John Sculley, former CEO of Apple

Computer, discussed his approach to fostering higher states of creativity within Apple in an interview in *Fortune* magazine:

> Defensiveness is the bane of all passion-filled creative work. We [at Apple] keep defenses down in several ways. One way is by thinking about problems differently—not as negatives, for example. We are thinking of giving people medals for problem finding, not just problem solving. Our world moves so fast that new problems are being created all the time. The people who find them have tremendous powers of creative observation.

Because mistakes are an inevitable outcome of risk-taking and creativity, we suggest that you examine the prevailing attitudes toward failure in your organizations to see more clearly what blocks or what supports leadership development and innovative problem-solving. To begin, you may want to conduct an organizational audit of the ways failures and mistakes are viewed. Conduct the audit for a defined period of time, for example, one week. Note every failure, problem, or mistake that you encounter during that time; observe whether you are responsible or someone else is "to blame"; and check to see whether the problem is seen as an opportunity for a creative solution. Sample issues to examine in conducting the audit are as follows:

A. Describe the failure or problem:

. . . .
. . . .
. . . .
. . . .

B. Indicate the points of view, attitudes, positions, and reactions taken by leadership toward the specified failure or problem:

. . . .

. . . .

. . . .

. . . .

C. Indicate how you see the problem, how you feel about it, and your reaction to it:

. . . .

. . . .

. . . .

. . . .

D. Describe an alternate point of view. Look for ways to see the failure as an opportunity, or as a learning experience, or as a means for putting a positive cast on the incident:

. . . .

. . . .

. . . .

. . . .

Though you can decide to involve others in this audit, make sure all the initial responses are your own. When you have completed the audit, share your results with colleagues from the organization, who may also have conducted one. Ask for feedback from others and compare your perceptions. Complete the checklist below, then use it as a reminder of how to view creativity and problem-solving.

Given the results of your audit and the insights you gained, you may want to use the checklist below to assess the creativity of your organization. In this exercise, you can practice taking a new attitude toward failure. In the checklist below, we first ask you to describe a problem in your organization. Next, we ask you to indicate the attitude toward the problem expressed by key people in the organization. The third column asks for your attitude regarding the problem. Note that it may be different from the one that is prevalent among your colleagues. Finally, we ask you to search for opportunities for creativity in solving the problem. In this last column you will have a chance to change your point of view about the problem, the solution, and your role in finding creative solutions. This change in perspective is one of the prerequisites to shifting your leadership paradigm. In this way, you can practice living in a new paradigm that includes recognizing the old paradigm, giving up old ways of thinking, creating alternate points of view, and adopting new behaviors.

The Creativity Checklist

Problem Description	Organizational Attitude	Your Attitude	Opportunity for Creativity
1.			
. . . .			
. . . .			
2.			
. . . .			
. . . .			
3.			
. . . .			
. . . .			
4.			
. . . .			
. . . .			

5.

. . . .

. . . .

6.

. . . .

. . . .

As you gain a new perspective on failure, you can stimulate significant changes in your organization. You can encourage your colleagues to revise their own thinking about their mistakes. In doing so, you can point out the creative solutions that can be found by learning from mistakes and using innovation and inspiration to generate alternatives.

Arnold Hiatt, retired chairman of Stride Rite Corporation—the successful U.S. footwear company—reported on his struggle to support people in learning from their mistakes. In the *Harvard Business Review* he said:

> My personal struggle has always been how far to let someone else go. I'll see someone in the company doing something I know isn't right, because I've been there myself too many times before. But then I grit my teeth and remind myself that I never learned anything by listening to someone else preach. The mistakes I made were my best teacher by far.

Learning, creativity, participation, innovation, flexibility, and communication are all by-products of an openness to mistakes, problems, and failures. The successful leaders of our times know that there are no scripts to follow, no cut-and-dried solutions to adopt. It is up to all of us to create the answers we need by working together and using our own resources. The discovery of solutions to the AIDS epidemic, the starvation of impoverished citizens, the gang warfare among our youth, and the homelessness of our urban populations will come from the lessons we learn from the failures we currently face.

Lessons from the Past—An Exercise

Knowing ourselves requires a knowledge of our history and an acknowledgment of our past. In an earlier exercise in this chapter, we explored our family histories and our models of leadership. In Chapter 3 we explored family legacies in greater detail. Now it is time to analyze the factors in our past experiences that shaped our view of ourselves as leaders to reveal the strengths we bring from those early experiences.

Our now departed friend and colleague, Will Schultz, developed an exercise for his book *The Human Element*. We include this powerful tool to deepen your awareness of your lessons from your past and enable you to see how they translate into your improved success as a leader.

• Either think about or draw a picture of yourself as far back as you can remember. Shut your eyes and picture yourself at your earliest age.

. . . .
. . . .
. . . .
. . . .

• In your family: What was your birth order? What was your role in your family's dynamics? How did you differ when your parents were at home, when they were not at home, when no one was at home?

. . . .
. . . .
. . . .
. . . .

• With your playmates: Were you a leader, dominant, shy, well-liked, ignored, rejected, admired, good at sports, good at school, a rebel?

. . . .

. . . .

. . . .

. . . .

• Was your size, your appearance, your gender, your race, your ethnic group a factor?

. . . .

. . . .

. . . .

. . . .

• Was there a change in your role when persons of the same or other gender were present, when dating began? Were you popular, unwanted, a loner, a party person, sought out, ignored? (*Reflect on how much of your current behavior regarding leadership is understandable in light of these early events.*)

. . . .

. . . .

. . . .

. . . .

• When you complete drawing or imagining this image, stand back and observe. What role have you typically played? At which roles are you most successful? With which are you likely to fail? Which do you enjoy? Which do you avoid?

. . . .

. . . .

. . . .

. . . .

• How do people typically treat you? In what ways do most people treat you the same way? In what ways do certain people treat you differently?

. . . .

. . . .

. . . .

. . . .

• How do you anticipate that people will respond to you when you first meet them? What types of reactions do you typically elicit—fatherly, flirtatious, sisterly, competitive, sympathetic, motherly, helper, victim, nasty, critical?

. . . .

. . . .

. . . .

. . . .

In reviewing your past experiences, there are rich lessons to be learned from understanding how you responded in your most difficult moments. As lifelong students of leadership, we are fascinated with the notion of what makes leaders. Why is it that certain people seem to naturally inspire confidence, loyalty, and hard work, while others (who may have just as much vision and smarts) stumble again and again? It's a timeless question—and there are no simple answers. But we have come to believe that whatever answers there are have something to do with the different ways people deal with adversity. Indeed, we have come to the conclusion that one of the most reliable indicators and predictors of effective leadership is an individual's ability to find meaning in negative events and learn even from the most trying circumstances. Put another way, the skills required to conquer adversity and emerge stronger and more committed than ever are the same ones that make for extraordinary leaders. Everyone is tested by life, but only a few extract strength and wisdom from their most trying experiences. They are the ones we call leaders.Warren's recent book with Robert J. Thomas (*Geeks and Geezers: How Ego, Values, and Defining Moments Shape Leaders*) describes in detail how outstanding leaders under the ages of thirty-five and over seventy faced what Warren calls the "crucibles" in their lives and how they prevailed in the challenges they met. We define "crucibles" as transformative experiences through which individuals come to a new or alternative sense of identity. All leaders face "crucible experiences" in which they are tested by the searing heat of life's disappointments, challenges, and tragedies. For instance, Mike Wallace, one of the leaders Warren interviewed, was shattered by the loss of his son. But this event became the turning point in his journalistic career, convincing him to take more risks and follow his passions. Some people are defeated by the challenges of the crucible, while others, like Wallace, come through transformed into significant leaders. Think of the manner in which alchemists used crucibles in hopes of turning ordinary things to gold; great leaders *are* that gold.

Here is a chance to reflect on how you would like to use the lessons you have learned, to confront the crucibles in your life, and to develop your strengths to forge yourself into a more effective leader.

Questions to Consider

A. What are the hardest lessons you have learned in your life? What are the crucibles that have been turning points in your life? How might they make you a better leader?

. . . .

. . . .

. . . .

B. Given your memories, describe the type of leader you could be that would make maximum use of your strengths and talents:

. . . .

. . . .

116

. . . .

. . . .

C. What are some ways you would like others to respond to you to continue to build your leadership capacity?

. . . .

. . . .

. . . .

. . . .

D. What experiences from the past do you need to overcome to be a more effective leader?

. . . .

. . . .

. . . .

. . . .

The process of knowing ourselves continues throughout our lives as we develop our leadership skills. New memories emerge from the recesses of our minds, and new insights about our past may arise. As they do, you may want to record them or save them for a time of reflection.

In Chapter 5, we shift from looking into the past to imagining the future and discovering the power of vision that enables the most successful leaders to create the support and the motivation they need to achieve their goals. Solutions to seemingly impossible problems grow from the dreams leaders have of what the future might be. Leaders are the initiators and communicators of powerful visions for change.

5 Creating and Communicating a Vision

All men dream; but not equally.

Those who dream by night in the dusty recesses of their minds

Awake to find that it was vanity;

But the dreamers of day are dangerous men,

That they may act their dreams with open eyes to make it possible.

T. E. Lawrence

ALTHOUGH LEADERS COME IN EVERY SIZE, SHAPE, AND DISPOSITION, THERE is at least one ingredient that every leader shares: passion for a guiding purpose, dedication to an overarching vision. Leaders are more than goal-directed, they are *vision-directed,* and like T. E. Lawrence's observation, they transform their visions from dreamlike fantasy into the harsh reality of life to bring them to fruition.

Leaders are the most results-oriented individuals in the world, and the results they produce get attention. They get results because their visions are compelling and pull people toward them. Their intensity, coupled with determination, is magnetic. With their explicit commitment to their vision, they do not have to coerce people to pay attention; they are so intent on what they are doing that, like a child completely absorbed with creating a sandcastle in a sandbox, they draw others in.

We think of it this way: *Leaders manage the dream.* All leaders have the capacity to dream and from their dreams, they create a compelling vision, one that takes people to a new place. Then they translate that vision into reality.

A Passionate Commitment to Vision

Vision *grabs*. Initially it grabs the leader, and her ability to communicate it enables others to get on her bandwagon.

Warren interviewed Sergio Comissioná, the renowned conductor, who was at that moment with the Houston Symphony Orchestra. For a long time he refused to be interviewed, which was remarkable in and of itself. He would not respond to letters; he would not answer phone calls. After many months, Warren was able to get in touch with two of his musicians. When asked what Comissioná was like, they answered, "Terrific." But when asked why, they wavered. Finally they said, "Because he does not waste our time."

That simple declarative sentence at first seemed insignificant. But it became clear from their explanation that Comissioná transmits an unbridled clarity to his players about what he wants from them. He knows precisely and emphatically what he wants to hear at any given time. This fixation with and undeviating attention to outcome—some would call it an obsession—is possible only if one knows what one wants. That can come only from vision or, as one member of Comissioná's orchestra referred to it, from "the maestro's tapestry of intentions." This passionate commitment to vision is described by a character from George Bernard Shaw's play *Man and Superman:*

> This is the true joy in life, the being used for a purpose recognized by yourself as a mighty one; the being a force of nature instead of a feverish selfish little clod of ailments and grievances complaining that the world will not devote itself to making you happy. I want to be thoroughly used up when I die, for the harder I work the more I live. I rejoice in life for its own sake. Life is

no "brief candle" to me. It is a sort of splendid torch which I have got hold of for the moment, and I want to make it burn as brightly as possible before handing it on to future generations.

There is a high, intense filament in our leaders, similar to Comissioná's passion about the "right" tone. Sometimes it burns only within the range of their vision. If they step outside that range they can be as dull or as interesting as anyone else. A basic ingredient of leadership is *passion*—the underlying passion for the promises of life, combined with a very particular passion for a vocation, a profession, a course of action. The leader loves what he does and loves doing it. As Tolstoy observed, hopes are the dreams of the waking man. Without hope, we cannot survive, much less progress. The leader who communicates passion gives hope and inspiration to others. Passion can be lived through enthusiasm, through vitality, and through a demonstrated and unswerving commitment to one's vision.

The Alignment of Others Through Meaning

If you can dream it, you can do it.

Walt Disney

This Disney quote figures high on a sign at the Epcot Center in Orlando, Florida. While it beckons the Don Quixote in all of us, believing in one's dreams is not enough. There are a lot of intoxicating visions and noble intentions that have come to naught. Many people have rich and deeply textured agendas, but without communication nothing can be realized. Success requires the capacity to communicate a compelling image of a desired state of affairs—the kind of image that induces enthusiasm and a commitment in others.

Leadership *is* a transaction between leaders and followers. Neither exists without the other. The interaction between leader and led is the simple truth: They each bring out the best in the other. This new style of leadership is an impressive and subtle sweeping back and forth of energy, whether between maestro and musicians, or CEO and staff. The transaction creates unity. Conductor and orchestra become one. Coach and team, leader and organization, become one. That unified focus results from the leader's skill in communicating a unifying vision.

As a leader, how do you capture the imagination of others? How do you communicate a vision? How do you get people aligned behind an organization's overarching goals? How do you get an audience to recognize and accept an idea? Effective leaders do so through the mastery of communication and the practice of empathy. Former CBS executive Barbara Corday prizes empathy, a skill she sees as comfortable for many women leaders:

> I think women generally see power in a different way than men. I don't have any need for personal power, especially over people. I want to have the kind of power that is my company working well, my staff working well. . . . As moms and wives and daughters we've been caretakers, and a lot of the caretakers in our lives were women, and we continue in caretaking roles even as we get successful in business. And that feels natural to us. I have always been very pleased and happy and proud of the fact that I not only know all the people who work for me, but I know their husbands' and wives' names, and I know their children's names, and I know who's been sick, and I know what to ask. That's what's special to me in a work atmosphere. I think that's what people appreciate, and that's why they want to be there, and that's why they're loyal, and that's why they care about what they're doing. And I think that is peculiarly female.

Empathy isn't only the province of women. Former Lucky Stores CEO Don Ritchey said,

I think one of the biggest turn-ons for people is to know that their peers and particularly their bosses not only know they're there but know pretty intimately what they're doing and are involved with them on almost a daily basis, that it's a partnership, that you're really trying to run this thing well together, that if something goes wrong our goal is to fix it, not see who we can nail.

Communicating with meaning is a required skill for leaders, if they want to realize their vision. Many leaders use metaphor to symbolize their vision and inspire others to implement it. For Charles Darwin, the metaphor was a branching tree of evolution on which he could trace the rise of various species. William James viewed mental processes as a stream or river. John Locke focused on the falconer, whose release of a bird symbolized his "own emerging view of the creative process."

When Frank Dale took over the *Los Angeles Herald-Examiner,* Los Angeles's afternoon newspaper, they were just ending a bloody 10-year strike. Dale, the new president and publisher, had to go in through the backdoor to greet his irksome staff because the front door was barred. Here are Dale's words in an interview with Warren:

It so happened that the front door of the building was barricaded. It had not been open in eight years. I had to walk through the back door, have my fingerprints taken, my picture taken: "Welcome aboard, boss!" I went to the newsroom within the first hour and asked the people who were working to come and gather around me so I could introduce myself. . . .

The lobby had been barricaded for over eight years. There was tremendous strife, people were killed, employees were killed and indeed, it was eventually some employees who had never been unionized or related to any union who simply said to each other over a beer one night: "We gotta quit shooting each other." And so, on a peace platform, they got the employees to vote for a settlement and eventually got the right to bargain. I called the people on duty at the time around the desk in an informal setting—I had no one to introduce me. . . . I did it myself so that I would be right there and without any forethought at all I said, "Maybe the first thing we ought to do is open up the front door." Everybody stood up and cheered. Grown men and women cried. That was a symbol, you see, that barricade was a symbol of defeat, of siege. And "let the sun in" was what I was saying. . . . And then I attempted to introduce myself again, thanked them for preserving the opportunity that I had been asked to take advantage of. Which is really what they did—when I let the sunshine in.

A number of lessons can be drawn from the experiences of leaders like Frank Dale who create meaning for others by powerfully communicating a compelling vision. First, *all* organizations depend on shared meanings and interpretations of reality to facilitate coordinated action. The actions and symbols of leadership frame and mobilize meaning. Leaders articulate and define what had previously remained implicit or unsaid; then they invent images, metaphors, and models that provide a focus for attention. By so doing, they consolidate or challenge prevailing wisdom. In short, an *essential* factor in leadership is the ability to influence and create *meaning* for the members of the organization.

What we mean by "meaning" goes far beyond what is usually meant by "communication." Meaning emerges from the process of thinking. Thinking prepares one for what is to be done, for what ought to be done. Thinking, though it may be unsettling and dangerous to the established order, is actually constructive: It challenges old conventions by suggesting new directions, new visions, new ways of doing things. The distinctive role of leadership, especially in our volatile environment, is to focus on "know-why" before "know-how." This distinction, once again, points to one of the key differences between leaders and managers.

What we see and experience on today's organizational landscape are cumbersome bureaucracies that more often than not demonstrate the mismanagement of meaning. In these environments where meaningful communication does not exist, a "great idea" may be hatched. Without leadership, responsibility for it is then delegated. Then it is delegated again. Then it is redelegated one or two more times. By the time this great idea is carried out, it is certainly not what the leader intended or anticipated. This "Pinocchio effect" is the bane of many creators who, like Gepetto the puppet maker, are confronted with distended, distorted versions of their original plans that have taken on a somewhat dishonest life of their own. Lack of clarity makes bureaucracies little more than mechanisms for evasion of both responsibility and leadership.

Communication creates meaning for people. Or it should. It is the only way any group, small or large, can become aligned behind the overarching goals of an organization. Getting the message across unequivocally at every level is absolutely key to producing *any* result—much less the one originally envisioned!

Your Organizational Vision—An Exercise

Leaders are the kind of people to whom others are drawn—not because of their personalities but because they have a dream, a vision, a set of intentions, an agenda, a frame of reference. Clearly, when we are with these individuals, we sense an extraordinary focus of commitment, which attracts us to them. It is often said of these leaders that they make us want to join with them: They enroll us in their vision.

By "vision" we mean a picture that can be seen with the mind's eye. We use "vision" rather than "mission" or "goals" because a vision can be *imagined*—it has substance, form, and color. Visual literacy experts tell us that the eye is the source of more than 85 percent of the information we take in. Our eyes are the direct portals to our minds. Leaders understand the power of the visual and use it to attract others to their dreams.

Your vision is a portrait of the future to which you and others can commit. It is the articulation of your ethics and values. It empowers you, inspires you to do your job, and motivates you to contribute ideas or actions beyond yourself. At this point, we would like to give you an opportunity to articulate a vision for yourself and share it with others. In this exercise, we ask you to create a vision both for your organization and for your job.

We suggest you begin by forming an encompassing organizational vision. To complete this exercise, look beyond your current position. From where you sit, you may see only a small piece of the action. Expand your view to include a vision for the entire organization—all the people, all the functions, all the results that are possible. The following criteria for your articulated vision can guide you in defining what you want to create:

- A vision engages your heart and your spirit.
- A vision taps into embedded concerns and needs.
- A vision asserts what you and your colleagues want to create.
- A vision is something worth going for.
- A vision provides meaning to the work of you and your colleagues.
- By definition a vision is a little cloudy and grand (if it were clear, it wouldn't be a vision).
- A vision is simple.
- A vision is a living document that can always be expanded.
- A vision provides a starting place from which to get to greater and greater levels of specificity.
- A vision is based in two deep human needs: quality and dedication.

Your vision will be uniquely your own. In creating it, we encourage you to take a risk: Be daring and reach for what you truly want for your organization and for your own role in it. Your vision should speak to the needs of others in the organization. It should also address the strivings and hopes that may be unexpressed but held strongly nonetheless. If it touches the deepest longings of your colleagues, if it resonates with what they actually feel, it will have power.

The following questions will enable you to form the images that will give power to your dreams. As you answer them, let the images flow. Do not censor yourself. Allow the poet and the dreamer in you to emerge. Eventually, after you have lived with your vision statement for a while, we suggest that you edit it to be brief, precise, and simple. Ultimately, it will be only a few sentences, no more than a paragraph, in using language that is vivid, clear, and communicative.

Questions to Consider

A. What is unique about your organization?

. . . .

. . . .

. . . .

. . . .

B. What are your values, and how do they shape your priorities for the future?

. . . .

. . . .

. . . .

. . . .

. . . .

. . . .

. . . .

. . . .

C. What do your customers, your clients, or the people you serve really need that you can provide?

. . . .

. . . .

. . . .

. . . .

. . . .

. . . .

. . . .

. . . .

D. What would make you personally commit your mind and heart to this vision over the next five to ten years?

. . . .

. . . .

. . . .

. . . .

E. What do you really want your organization to accomplish so that you will feel committed, aligned, and proud of your association with it?

. . . .

. . . .

. . . .

. . . .

. . . .

. . . .

. . . .

. . . .

Now that you have answers to these preliminary questions, you will be ready to begin shaping your vision. There are several steps that will support you in creating your vision. Start with your dream for the entire organization. Think big—draw a picture for the whole institution. Later, you will create a vision for your own work that you can bring into alignment with your larger vision for the whole.

1. To be fully supported, find a place to work that is comfortable. Perhaps you have a special room at home or an area of the office where you can think and where you have privacy. Some people like to envision in a quiet, natural setting. Others work best over a cup of cappuccino at a favorite coffee house. Select a spot that is most conducive to leaving the present behind and projecting yourself into the future.

2. Clear your mind of present-day obstacles and difficulties. As soon as your mind starts to dream of the future, the part of your brain that is grounded in reality will kick in and tell you that you are being unrealistic, foolish, slothful, or embarrassing. Ask this reality-checking function to be quiet for now and request permission to allow yourself to go as far as you can with your hopes and wishes.

3. Each of us has our own way of being creative. Some of us do not know what we think until we say it. Others need time to listen to our inner voice to see the future of which dreams are made and to write about it. The artists among us may feel more comfortable drawing a sketch of what the future may look like. Some of us may want to simply close our eyes and dream. Choose your own approach. As you picture the next five or ten years into the future, consider these questions:
   - What are characteristics of the international stage for action?
   - How does your organization fit in this changed environment?
   - What does it contribute?
   - How is it viewed by others?
   - How does it feel to live inside this organization?
   - What does it look like physically?
   - How many people work there?
   - What products and services does it deliver?

4. What do you wish for your organization in the future? You may want to close your eyes to get a deeper image of your vision. You may want to start writing and see what emerges. It may be more useful to talk to someone else as you begin this work.

5. As your vision begins to unfold, capture it on paper or on a tape recorder, or draw it on large sheet of paper, or write it as a narrative in the space provided on these pages. You may prefer to present it to a friend and have your friend take notes. As it starts to emerge, develop it, let it expand and fill out until it is complete. Do not edit or censor your vision—let it flow until you have created the images that are right for you.

6. Now that you have articulated an image, go back and review the questions above to make sure you have fully developed all aspects of your vision. Then go back over it again to tighten the language and make it clear, simple, compelling, concise and complete.

The vision you have just crafted should be thought of as a living document. It is meant to be shared with others, tested in conversations, and presented to colleagues for their reactions. Find opportunities to present your vision to those you want to inspire. If you are working in a team, have each person share his or her vision. Look for common qualities. Identify major differences. Negotiate the differences and create a shared vision with which everyone can identify.

Your Vision for Your Organization

. . . .

. . . .

. . . .

. . . .

. . . .

. . . .

. . . .
. . . .
. . . .
. . . .
. . . .
. . . .
. . . .
. . . .
. . . .
. . . .
. . . .
. . . .
. . . .
. . . .
. . . .
. . . .
. . . .
. . . .
. . . .

If you are working as a team, you will find it valuable to have a team vision. Use the same process to create a team vision by working together to answer the questions above. As a team, you may want to communicate your vision to others in the organization. Your purpose should *not* be to give them your ideas as the "right" vision but to inspire them to envision the future for themselves and to add to your formulation. As a leader you may want to involve others in creating or revising your vision. Ask them what they think of it. How would they change it? Does it excite and inspire them? You can be a model for them in creating their own vision or allowing them to find their place in yours.

A Vision for Yourself—An Exercise

Now that you have created a vision for your organization, it is appropriate to place yourself inside this image. Dare to envision yourself as you truly want to be. Leadership means not only having a dream but claiming that dream and the role you want to play in living it. Arlene Blum, leader of a woman's expedition to climb the Himalayas, has written beautifully about the power of her vision. At 3:29 P.M. on October 15, 1978, a team of ten women became the first American climbing team to reach the summit of Annapurna I, the tenth-highest mountain in the world. Arlene Blum was the leader of the expedition. She and her partners created a vision for themselves that challenged all the traditional expectations that a male-dominated society has of women. The entire expeditionary team not only believed that women could climb the Himalayas but owned this vision themselves and made it happen.

> As women, we faced a challenge even greater than the mountain. We had to believe in ourselves enough to make the attempt in spite of social convention and two hundred years of climbing history in which women were usually relegated to the sidelines.

Blum wrote about how women had been told for years that they were not strong enough to carry heavy loads, and that they didn't have the leadership experience or emotional stability necessary to climb the highest mountains.

> Our expedition would give ten women the chance to attempt one of the world's highest and most challenging peaks, as well as the experience necessary to plan future Himalayan climbs. If we succeeded, we would be the first

Americans to climb Annapurna and the first American women to reach eight thousand meters (26,200 feet).

Blum and her team challenged two hundred years of assumptions to create the vision they ultimately achieved. We invite you to be as daring in your vision for yourself as they had the courage to be.

The following exercise will support you in getting to the heart of your dreams. It has been adapted from a leadership course developed by our colleagues Beth Jandernoa and Alain Gauthier, in which they enable participants to create visions for their personal future.

You will remember the Guided Imaging exercise in Chapter 4. We will repeat it now to enable you to gain access to your innermost creativity. If you are working with a partner, ask your colleague to read the relaxation instructions to you so you can clear your mind of extraneous thoughts and feelings. After you have completed the experience, you can repeat the process for your partner by reading the instructions to him or her. If you are working alone, read the instructions, then close your eyes and repeat them as best you can. You need not worry about getting all the instructions right. The purpose of the exercise is for you to relax and let go of everything that may be obstructing your vision.

Guided Imaging Instructions

Sit in a comfortable position with your back against a chair and your feet firmly on the floor. [Pause.] Good.

Uncross your legs and hands and rest them in a relaxed position in your lap. [Pause.] Good.

Gently let your eyes close. Easily take several deep breaths and slowly release them. [Pause.] With each breath let your eyes relax and let your body release any tension that is there. [Pause.] Good.

Notice any sounds or movements in the room and release your attention from these sounds and movements. [Pause.] Good.

Let any thoughts you have come into your consciousness, and then release these thoughts. [Pause.] Good.

Let any emotions you have come into your consciousness, and then release these emotions. [Pause.] Good.

Let any pictures from the past come into your consciousness, and then release these pictures from the past. [Pause.] Good.

Now you are sitting comfortably in your chair. [Pause.] You have let go of any noises or movements in the room. [Pause.] You have released all your tensions, thoughts, emotions, and pictures from your past. [Pause.] Good.

Now focus your attention on your feet and legs. If there is any tension there, release it. [Pause.] Good.

Now focus your attention on your abdomen and lower body. If there is any tension there, release it. [Pause.] Good.

Now focus your attention on your chest, shoulders, and arms. If there is any tension there, release it. [Pause.] Good.

Now focus your attention on your neck, head, and face. If there is any tension there, release it. [Pause.] Good.

Now you are fully relaxed and open to whatever is there for you. [Pause.] Good.

Now let go of all the images you have had in your mind, and just relax. [Pause.] Good.

Remain in a relaxed, peaceful place. [Pause.] Just let any feelings, thoughts, or pictures come to the surface and release them.

Now begin to feel the back of the chair next to your body and the floor under your feet. [Pause.] Good.

Begin to return your attention to the room. [Pause.] Good.

Begin to hear the noises in the room. [Pause.] Notice any movement in the room. [Pause.] Good.

As I count to five, return your attention to the room. One. [Pause.] Two. [Pause.] Three. [Pause.] Four. [Pause.] Five. [Pause.] Open your eyes, and say hello to someone here in the room. Thank you.

Now that you are relaxed and comfortable you can begin to create your personal vision. Remember to use a form of expression that is natural for you. Thinking and imagining to yourself, talking with a partner, writing or recording a narrative, drawing or sculpting are all possible forms. The following questions will guide you in creating your personal vision. Some may not apply to you. Feel free to disregard irrelevant questions. We may not have included others that may be relevant in sparking your creativity. Use these questions as a starting point for your envisioning process. It may be helpful to close your eyes after reading each section and let the answers come to you first without thinking about whether they are useful.

Self
Start by imagining yourself living to your full potential, demonstrating all your talents, enjoying your strengths, being in your prime and at your peak. What are the qualities you possess? How do you feel about yourself? What are you doing? How are you living? What brings you joy and happiness?

Health
Consider your health. Imagine the kind of health you want for yourself. Include emotional, physical, mental, and spiritual health in your vision. Imagine how you will maintain a healthy life. What kind of activities and thoughts can help you achieve and continue your vision of health?

Relationship
Think of your closest relationship. Imagine a conversation that would best symbolize this relationship at its highest level. What do you hear, see, feel? Focus on the qualities you bring to this relationship. What do you offer the other person? What are the two of you doing? How are you contributing to each other? Repeat this process with other important relationships.

Family
Bring your family into your vision. How do they seem to you? What are they doing? How has your relationship with them evolved? Notice their health

and well-being. What is most satisfying to you about your relationship with them? How are you contributing to each other? What is your greatest source of joy in your relationship with them?

Work Life
Focus now on your work life. Take a long-term perspective and consider the vision you have created for your organization. How would you express what really matters to you in your work? What is the quality of your day-to-day life? How can it be improved? How have you demonstrated your values? What have you achieved? What gives you the greatest sense of satisfaction? What rewards are available to you? What is the culmination of your contribution?

Community Contributions
Consider the individuals, families, schools, and social institutions in your community that could benefit from your talents. Picture the contributions you could make to improve your community and society. What could you give to those who are in need? How satisfying and rewarding could your social contributions be to you, as well as those who receive the benefits? Picture how you might make a difference in your community.

Enriching Activities
Now look at your personal hobbies, adventures, and volunteer commitments that fulfill your personal aspirations. Imagine having all the enjoyable, satisfying, and contributing aspects of your life in your vision. What are these activities? What do you bring to them? What do they contribute to enriching and rounding out your life?

After you have answered these questions in a form that is most comfortable for you, take a look at all the elements of a life vision that emerged. How do all these pieces fit together? What does the whole picture look like? Are there aspects that are in conflict with one another? Does your vision form a coherent whole? Does it please and inspire you? Is it a vision worth your commitment and energy? In the space provided, write your completed vision for your life as a short essay.

Your Vision for Yourself

. . . .

. . . .

. . . .

. . . .

. . . .

. . . .

. . . .

. . . .

. . . .

. . . .

. . . .

. . . .

. . . .

. . . .

. . . .

. . . .

. . . .

. . . .

. . . .

. . . .

. . . .

. . . .

Communicating Your Vision—An Exercise

Your vision will become a powerful force for change only if you communicate it to others in ways that are accessible and inspiring to them. The next step in transforming a dream into reality is to communicate your vision to others.

Communicating your vision requires attention and conscious planning. We often communicate as though we are talking to a mirror image of ourselves, not realizing that those we intend to inspire have concerns different from our own. When leaders understand their followers and communicate with them using that understanding, their followers understand those who lead. Former Senator John Tunney of California described Robert Kennedy's talent for creating a magical connection through communicating a vision—and the results he produced in those he touched:

> His sense of politics was physical, in that he knew you had to throw yourself out there among the people again and again, to be directly heard and seen and touched and sort of handled and pushed around by them. There's a huge hunger to connect to an actual physical presence—a tribal leader, really, with that kind of personal relationship between him and the people—who can give them a sense of meaning and value as a community again. It's something almost primitive, mystic.

Both John and Robert Kennedy brilliantly translated their visions into a physical presence and a vivid, inspiring language that touched many people. Those who were willing to follow the dream they articulated did so because the dream was communicated in ways that made it real for them.

In this exercise, we ask you to capture this quality for yourself by planning how you will communicate your organizational vision. Your challenge will be to communicate it powerfully and with inspiration so that others embrace and support it. Tunney describes how Robert Kennedy "has almost recklessly, with a willingness to take extraordinary risks, given himself over completely to what he believes in, which answers what they believe in." Your presentation of your vision should have the following qualities: It should express your excitement, love for, and commitment to your dream; it should be clear and vivid and reach others with the magic you create.

In presenting your vision, make it engaging and inspiring. You can even use drawings, a song, poetry, a skit, or a narrative story, to involve others. In planning your presentation, think about your audience and speak to *their* needs, in order to fire them up, reach their hearts, excite them with your dream while at the same time do not fall into the trap of a demagogue who is more interested in the audience's response than in the integrity of his vision.

With this exercise, you have an opportunity to develop your communication skills. If you have been working alone, invite a small group of colleagues or friends to assist you. Invite them to hear or see your vision and discuss it with you. Set the stage by asking them to set aside today's realities and visit the future with you. If you are already on a team or part of a larger group, continue with them as your vision partners. If your colleagues have also created visions for the organization, have them present their visions as well. Let them know that you really value their reactions.

A. After the presentation(s), the tendency will be for everyone to want to discuss what the vision *said*. Try to postpone that conversation and first focus on *how* it was communicated; with this discussion you and everyone else can become more effective in using the power of communication, as well as the force of the vision itself.

B. Notice the differences in each person's communication. Elicit feedback about what was effective or problematic about each presentation.

C. *Now* discuss the substance of the vision(s). If several were presented for the same organization, notice the differences and discuss the basis of each difference.

D. Look for commonalties in everyone's vision statement. Try to create a group vision for the future of the organization. This exercise can contribute to building a stronger team as everyone shares a common vision.

E. If you are the only person with a vision, work with the group so they can accept it as their own. Have them discuss the parts of the vision they like and suggest changes in the parts that do not satisfy them.

F. Consider making a presentation of your vision to a special group within the organization: a group of clients, managers, secretaries, or outside vendors. How would you change your communication to speak to these diverse interest groups?

As others work with your vision statement, you will want to allow them to make the changes they wish. Avoid becoming defensive. Let them make it their own by changing it and adding whatever they think is needed for them to feel it is theirs. Stay true to your basic principles, but let them rework the language and ideas so that everyone can buy in to it.

Sharing your personal vision with others is the final step in the visioning process. If you do not feel ready to present your personal vision to colleagues, share it with family members who are closest to you. Think about how your personal vision compares with your organizational vision. Is there dissonance between the two? Are they equally clear and compelling? If not, why not? Try again, and then incorporate ideas from one into the other. Ask your friends and family for their reactions and support. Let them create a vision for themselves. Allow your vision to become theirs or have theirs integrated into yours.

Jesse Jackson, a master visionary and communicator, describes his early years when he began to share his dreams. Quoted in a *New Yorker* portrait by Marshall Frady, this complex, riveting orator talked about how he learned to communicate a vision to reach the hearts of others.

When I first came back home from the seminary, I was asked to speak at church, and my grandmother and some of the older folk came up afterward. "That was a nice speech, young man, very nice speech." They meant the words were. Words came out nice. That's what it was, a speech. But as you go on and begin to really catch hold of it, you start hearing them say, "Well, now. You spoke to my soul. You burned me this morning." Got to do more than *speak*. You can get informed listening to a newsman or weatherman. You got to be moving toward the heart of the matter, got to burn people's souls. You got to get *inside* of people. That's where it all is. And you can't get inside of them unless you open *yourself* up to be got inside *of*. Follow what I'm saying? The key to other people's hearts is finding the key to yours. Got to give to receive, got to open up yourself to get inside somebody else.

Jackson's message to us is this: When we create and communicate visions directly from our hearts, we directly connect with the hearts of others, causing them to want to join us in reaching our dreams, because they share these dreams as well. Translating your vision into reality is the next task to learn in becoming a leader. In Chapter 6, you will learn the key to doing this by building trusting relationships between leaders and followers. These relationships will transform visions into vibrant realities.

6 Maintaining Trust Through Integrity

Trust, is fragile. Like a piece of china, once cracked it is never quite the same. And people's trust in business, and those who lead it, is today cracking. To many, it seems that executives no longer run their companies for the benefit of consumers, or even of their shareholders and employees, but for their personal ambition and financial gain. A Gallup poll conducted early this year found that 90% of Americans felt that people running corporations could not be trusted to look after the interest of their employees, and only 18% thought that corporations look after their shareholders a great deal. Forty-three percent, in fact, believed that senior executives were only in it for themselves. In Britain, that figure, according to another poll was 95%.

Charles Handy, "What's a Business For?" *Harvard Business Review*, December 2002

WHY DID INDIA'S POOR MARCH TO THE SEA WITH GANDHI AGAINST the salt tax? What was it about Margaret Sanger that emboldened women to break with husbands and families and adopt birth control? What did Dr. Martin Luther King Jr. do to inspire poor, uneducated sharecroppers who were tied to the soil of the American South to register to vote? We know that each of these leaders believed in the correctness of his or her cause at a moment in history when action was called for. Their impact was profound because the trust they enjoyed was based on invincible integrity and powerful commitment. Trust is the essential quality that creates a following for leaders and enables them to make a difference. It is the key ability that inspires those who join them to create movements for social change and build organizations to realize their dreams.

We want and need leaders we can trust. Trust is a whole lot harder to come by than competence, which is why we have so many more managers than leaders. Unlike competence, trust can't be acquired by would-be leaders but can only be voluntarily given by their followers.

Our perception of a leader's performance is more important than her actual performance. In general, the people we trust "walk their talk." And when they do, what they espouse is what they do, and what they espouse and do is in synch with what we want and need. Leaders we trust are there when we need them, and they are on our side. They can perform the functions of the office and have a kind of steadiness, or "trusted thumb." They are able to control themselves in difficult situations, and under pressure, they do not act recklessly.

Leaders don't care a whit about posterity or even wonder how they'll be remembered. They do what needs to be done as well as they can do it, without a thought as to what the media will say about them today, or what historians will say about them ten years from now. They neither grandstand nor suffer from delusions of grandeur.

Leaders are ambitious, or they wouldn't have made it to the top, but they are ambitious for all of us, and they trust us as much as we trust them. Such leaders are so good a what they do that they bring out the best in us.

Trust and Organizational Effectiveness

Trust provides the motivation and energy that makes it possible for organizations to be successful. It is hard to imagine an institution in which leaders do not inspire some semblance of trust. It is what motivates heroism, sells products, and keeps communication humming. Trust is the source of organizational integrity.

Like leadership, trust is hard to describe, let alone define. We know when it is present, and we know when it is not. We are aware that it is essential and that it is based on predictability. We trust people who are predictable, whose positions are known and who keep at it; leaders who are trusted make themselves known and make their positions clear. Organizations without trust would resemble the nightmare of Kafka's *Castle*, where nothing can be certain and no one can be relied on or held accountable. The ability to predict the outcomes of leadership with a high probability of success generates and maintains trust.

In this chapter we explore trust by focusing on the four qualities of leadership that, when practiced, engender trust: Having a clear, articulate vision; practicing consistent empathy; behaving with reliable consistency; and acting with impeccable integrity. A leader who is trusted demonstrates these four characteristics:

- Trusted leaders have inspiring *visions* for the organization that are clear, attractive, and attainable. Their vision provides a context of shared beliefs and a common organizational purpose with which we can identify. As a result we feel that we belong. The leader involves us in their vision, empowers us to make it real, and enables us to integrate it into our lives.
- Trusted leaders have unconditional *empathy* for those who live in their organizations. We tend to trust leaders who can walk in our shoes and are able to let us know that. Although they may have different points of view, they can see the world as we see it and understand the sense we are making of it.
- The behaviors of trusted leaders are consistent with their values and the *commitments* they have. We tend to trust leaders when we know where they stand in relation to their organizations, as well as how they seek to orient their organizations in relation to the larger environment. We understand how these leaders' commitments have evolved and we know they are willing to reconsider them in the face of new evidence.
- The *integrity* of trusted leaders is unquestionable. We tend to trust leaders who stand for a higher moral order and who demonstrate their ethics and

values through actions we can observe. Leaders uphold a standard of ethics, encourage others to act on their shared values, and call themselves and others to account for deviations from what they know is right.

Qualities of Leadership—An Exercise

We begin our exploration of trust with an exercise that enables you to explore your relationships with leaders who exhibit the four qualities associated with trust. As you may remember from your work in earlier chapters, self-reflection and awareness are keys to your continued learning. In becoming a leader, you will want to commit to being trustworthy and aligning your actions with your values. Reflection is the initial step in doing so. As you think about your own behavior, you can evaluate your track record in matching your actions with the values to which you are committed. The purpose of this exercise is to give you an opportunity to reflect on the qualities of leadership that elicit trust so that they are explicit and you are more aware of them in others and in yourself.

To begin, refer back to Chapter 1 and the list of leaders you identified who inspired your life. This list, together with any additions you may want to make, constitutes the people whom you will consider in this exercise.

A. You may want to review your list and add the names of others you have remembered. Eliminate the people you have come to consider managers rather than leaders. Number each person so you can place them on the diagram below.

B. The following diagram is a *socio-gram* that graphs social relationships. Begin by placing yourself at the center of the hub. Now add the names of leaders on the lines that project out from the hub. The length of each line should vary to indicate the social distance between yourself and the particular leader designated by the line. For example, if you consider Gloria

Steinem an important leader and do not know her personally, put her on a line that is a long distance from the center, such as Leader #4 in the diagram. If one of the leaders on your list is the man who leads your son's Boy Scout troop and you consider him a close friend, place him close to you, such as Leader #2. If you consider yourself a leader, create a number for yourself on the chart at the hub.

C. Reflect on the social distance of each person in the diagram from your position at the hub. What do you notice about the relationship between your position and that of others? What relationships do you notice among the various leaders on the chart? Are there any surprises? Do you notice any patterns? Observe the distance of the leaders from you. Is the length of these distances associated with gender, race, age, social class, sexual orientation, or role?

D. Next, add the qualities of leadership that engender trust to the chart. In the space on the diagram beside each leader's number place the following designations:

V for those leaders who have and are able to express an inspiring personal and professional *vision*;
E for those leaders who demonstrate the ability to *empathize*;
C for those leaders who have clear and consistent *commitments* and use them to orient the organization;
I for those leaders who demonstrate *integrity* through values and ethical practices.

For example, if former Secretary of Defense Clark Clifford, long considered an American leader, were on your list, he might have a *V* for being a visionary, and a *C* for consistency of commitments to himself and his organization. However, subsequent to his government service, he was a director of the BCCI bank, which was embroiled in scandals that revealed the complicity of Clifford and other banking leaders in fraud and corruption. Thus, he may not have an *I* for integrity or an *E* for empathizing with the people who lost their savings due to the bank's dealings. On the other hand, if Marian Wright Edelman, founder of the Children's Defense Fund and long-time advocate for children in poverty, is on your list, as a woman of vision, with deep empathy for the poor, who exhibits high integrity and whose commitments are crystal-clear, she might have all four letters next to her name. When you analyze the leaders you have selected, your chart might look like the one below.

E. Once you have created your chart, reflect on it. What do you notice? Who are the leaders with integrity? Is there a pattern regarding leaders with vision? Are the leaders who are closest to you the ones who have empathy? Do the leaders on your chart have all the elements of trust, or are they missing some?

F. Notice the relationships among the leaders you diagramed. Connect the lines among the leaders who know each other. Do you notice any patterns among them? Who are the leaders who are connected? Do they have characteristics in common?

G. If you are working with a team, share your socio-gram with others. You need not mention names if you would rather not reveal the identity of those on your diagram. Discuss the patterns you notice with your team members. If you are willing to share names, discuss whether some members of your group have the same people on their charts or placed them in different positions with different assessments. Notice if you or others on your team are on someone else's chart as a leader. If you are on a chart, what characteristics have been assigned to you? If you aren't on a chart, what might you have to do to be put there?

H. What do you notice about trust? Who are the leaders on your chart you trust more than others? What are the characteristics that matter to you? Do you trust someone more if they empathize with you, or is their integrity more important to you? What does this exercise tell you about your own values?

Socio-Gram of Social Relations with Leaders

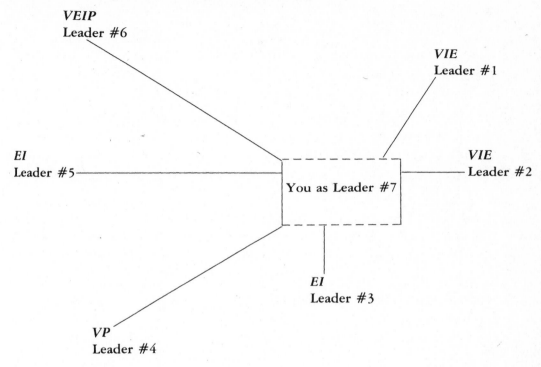

As we continue our exploration of trust, we will investigate the concepts of vision, empathy, commitment, and integrity in greater depth. As we do so, you may want to return to your socio-gram to refine your perspective on the leaders in your life.

Support Through Empathy

A basic ingredient of leadership is a guiding vision. Leaders who are trusted have a clear idea of what they want to do both professionally and personally.

They draw on their vision to give themselves and their followers the strength to persist in the face of setbacks, even failures. Unless they know where they are going and why, they cannot possibly get there, and if they are not inspired they will give up. Thus a vision for the future is crucial to producing any *strategic* result at all.

As you recall, in Chapter 5 we addressed the importance of the leader's skill in being able to effectively create and communicate a vision. You may want to review your vision and the comments you garnered to remind yourself of the power of an articulated vision. If leaders only have a vision, however, they may end up successfully prophesizing the future yet they may feel frustrated, lonely, and ineffectual. Leaders cannot achieve their dreams without recruiting people to support their vision. How do they do that? Ultimately, the ability of leaders to galvanize coworkers resides both in a clear understanding of themselves as well as the needs and wants of coworkers, and a strong, abiding belief in their mission to lead. Sydney Pollack, the successful film director, described a leader's ability to bring people to his side this way:

> Up to a point, I think you can lead out of fear, intimidation, as awful as that sounds. You can make people follow you by scaring them, and you can make people follow by having them feel obligated. You can lead by creating guilt. There is a lot of leadership that comes out of fear dependence, and guilt. The marine boot camp is famous for it. But the problem is that you're creating obedience with a residue of resentment. If you want to make a physics analogy, you'd be moving through the medium but you'd be creating a lot of drag, a lot of backwash. There are two other qualities that I think are more positive reasons to follow someone. One is an honest belief in the person you're following. The other is selfish. The person following has to believe that following is the best thing to do at the time. I mean it has to be apparent to them that they are getting something better by following you than they ever would by not following you. You don't want people to follow you just because that's what they're paid for. Sometimes you can teach them something. "You're

going to learn more by doing this movie than you would by doing another movie" let's say. You try to make everyone feel they have a stake in it.

Visionary leaders invite people to feel they have a stake in realizing the vision. They empower them to experience the vision as their own. They offer opportunities to join them and create their own visions. They explore what the vision will mean to their jobs and lives. They envision a future that clarifies the purpose and values of the organization. They have the ability to connect with others and at the same time they see them as separate from themselves. In some deeper sense, they know that they are also alike. This ability is an expression of the leader's capacity for empathy.

Our friend and colleague Dr. Norman Paul, a leading psychiatrist, believes empathy is a key to successful relationships. In his essay "Parental Empathy" he describes the qualities that are necessary for empathetic leadership:

> Empathy is different from sympathy; the two processes are, in fact, mutually exclusive. In sympathy, the subject is principally absorbed in his own feelings as they are projected into the object and has little concern for the reality and validity of the object's special experience. Sympathy bypasses real understanding of the other person, and that other is denied his own sense of being. Empathy, on the other hand, presupposes the existence of the object as a separate individual, entitled to his own feelings, ideas and emotional history. The empathizer makes no judgments about what the other *should* feel, but solicits the expression of whatever he *does* feel and, for brief periods, experiences these feelings as his own. The empathizer oscillates between such subjective involvement and a detached recognition of the shared feelings. The periods of his objective detachment do not seem to the other to be spells of indifference, as they would in sympathy; they are, instead, evidence that the subject respects himself and the object as separate people. Secure in his sense of self and his own emotional boundaries, the empathizer attempts to nurture a similar security in the other.

Most of us know when a leader with whom we interact is able to empathize with us. We experience being understood on a deep level. It feels as though we are more than understood—we are *known*. But empathetic leaders do not merge with us or violate our personal boundaries. They do not take away our feelings or responses. They do not overpower us with the resonance they have with us. An empathetic leader is able to acknowledge who we are and walk in our shoes.

Practicing Empathy—An Exercise

Learning to empathize means making a conscious effort to listen to the other person and hear what she is saying in the context of *her own* orientation, needs, and perceptions. When you empathize, your attention is on the other person rather than on yourself. Letting other people know you empathize with their situation, their position, their feelings means:

- Feeding back to them what you hear them say or see them do;
- Asking them questions to learn more about what they really feel or believe;
- Repeating their comments back to show them you have heard them without inserting your own ideas; and
- Understanding their point of view from the inside out, as though it were your own.

An empathic leader does not judge the responses of others or stifle them with his own agenda. Rather, the leader listens to the other person in silence, gives her the space to have her own reactions, and lets her know that she has been heard.

In the exercise that follows, you will have an opportunity to practice your skills in empathy. It is easy to empathize with someone you like, someone with whom you identify, or someone who is taking a position you admire. It is more difficult to practice empathy with someone who is disagreeable or creates problems. The following case study offers a challenge because Ed, the person described, exhibits difficult behaviors. In reading his story, you may not like what the protagonist says or does. You may find yourself getting annoyed or exasperated. If you have these reactions they will allow you to test your empathy and see if you can understand him as though he were you.

Our case study concerns Ed. We present his history from the perspective of his boss, Baxter, someone who needs and wants to empathize with Ed, so Ed can learn new behavior and save his job. See if you can get underneath his behavior to distinguish what is happening on the surface from what is taking place at a deeper level. Find a space within yourself from which you can start to understand Ed. After reading the case, complete the exercise.

Ed was born of working-class parents in Brooklyn, New York. Smart, ambitious, determined to succeed, he went to work in a factory right out of high school, then he enrolled in night school at a community college. Working day and night, he managed to earn a degree in accounting. With his new credential he moved off the factory floor and into management in the same manufacturing firm. Within a few short years, he had worked his way up the ladder, passing people with MBAs along the way. He proved himself to be not only hard-working and aggressive but a talented nuts-and-bolts employee. Efficient, competent, and tough, he eventually made Vice President.

Ed was a company man. Everyone said so. He not only knew how everything worked, he was capable of making it work better, and when necessary he took on difficult jobs that nobody wanted. He didn't seem to mind firing staff or "yanking out the deadwood" as he termed it. He was not an easy man to work for. He lacked the ability to communicate effectively with those who worked for him. You never heard a "well done" or "good job," you only heard complaints. But he was just the kind of man his bosses liked. He was 100 percent loyal to the company, a workaholic, always willing and eager to go that extra mile, and impatient with anyone who was less devoted.

Ed's competence, combined with his drive and toughness, made him an ideal executive in the win-or-die 1990s. To look at him or see him in action, no one would ever have guessed that he grew up poor on the streets of South Brooklyn, or that he was a night-school product.

In fact, he'd nearly forgotten it himself. He looked, dressed, and talked like his bosses. He had an attractive, devoted wife who looked, dressed, and talked like his bosses' wives. He had two handsome, well-behaved sons, a nice house in Westchester, a wicked tennis serve, and great prospects—if he wanted to move. The President of his company was in his early fifties, the same age as Ed, and not going anywhere; he was happy with his position. There was no room at the top for Ed in the foreseeable future.

About the time Ed began getting restless, a family-owned firm in the same industry was looking for new blood. The CEO, the grandson of the founder, was thinking of retirement, and there was no one to whom he could hand over the reins. This CEO wanted to bring someone in as a Vice President, get to know him, and if all went well, turn the firm over to him within two or three years. Although the firm was based in Minneapolis, an executive search firm found Ed in New York. Ed saw the move to Minneapolis as his shortcut to the top.

He handled the job-hop as efficiently as he handled everything else. He moved his family into a bigger and better house in Edina, moved himself into a big corner office with a view of a lake, and seemed to adjust to the slower Midwestern rhythm without missing a beat.

Yet with this move, he became, if anything, tougher than before, coming down harder than ever on people who failed to please him. He often exploded, giving vent to his anger, and sometimes blamed others for his own mistakes. The more relaxed Minnesotans in the office made fun of him privately and nicknamed him "the Brooklyn Bomber," but when he said jump, they jumped.

After Ed had been in Minneapolis about a year, Baxter, the CEO, took him to lunch and offered him the COO (chief operating officer) spot. Ed was pleased but not surprised. No one worked harder than he did, no one could have learned more about the company than he had, and no one deserved the promotion more. The sky was the limit for the Bomber now. Baxter and Ed were a great team. Baxter, genial and encouraging, steered the company, while Ed, tougher than ever, took care of the nuts and bolts and dirty work.

Baxter decided that Ed was indeed the fellow to replace him when he retired and announced his decision to the family, who comprised the Board of Directors. For the first time in his life, Ed ran into something he couldn't tough his way through. Some members of the family board told Baxter that Ed was *too* tough, *too* rough on his fellow executives. They would not approve of his appointment unless Ed could improve his "people skills."

Baxter gave Ed the bad news. If Ed was disturbed—and he was—so was his CEO. Baxter was ready to retire, had chosen Ed as his successor, and had begun to groom him for the job. Now his orderly succession plan had fallen apart.

After a while, it became clear everything everyone said about Ed was true. He was very competent and very ambitious, but he was also a tyrant. He was impulsive and frequently abusive of people who worked for him. They actually cowered in his presence. He had a desperate need to control both people and events. He was incapable of thanking anyone for a job well done, and he couldn't give a compliment. He was also a sexist and did not treat the women who worked under him as professionals.

Your task in this exercise is to coach Ed on what he should do to gain the CEO position he wants and develop a different, yet satisfactory, strategy for success. To be useful to Ed and effective in advising him, you must first empathize with him and his situation so he does not become defensive and resist your leadership. The following questions may help you deepen your empathy for his predicament:

Questions to Consider

A. What are Ed's insecurities and fears? What is their origin in his past history and current life?

. . . .

. . . .

B. What has he contributed to the company in the past?

. . . .

. . . .

C. What personal price has he paid to play the game by the handed-to-him rules?

. . . .

. . . .

D. How does Ed feel now that his climb to the top has been thwarted?

. . . .

. . . .

E. What are some questions he should ask himself as his game plan unravels and he considers how to succeed?

. . . .

. . . .

As you reflect on Ed's situation and put yourself in his shoes, try to answer the following questions for yourself:

A. When have you been in Ed's shoes in your life?

. . . .

. . . .

B. How did you feel?

. . . .

. . . .

C. What did you do with those feelings?

. . . .

. . . .

D. How did others react?

. . . .

. . . .

E. How would you have felt if you had been told by Baxter about the Board's decision?

. . . .

. . . .

Now create a scenario for a coaching session with Ed. If you are working with a team, you may want to role-play the scene in which you play Ed's coach while another member of your team plays Ed. The person who most dislikes Ed should role-play him, so he has a chance to see what it feels like to live in Ed's skin. This will give the person playing Ed an expanded opportunity to practice empathy!

If you are working alone, write out your dialogue. In writing, you can play all parts: the boss, coach, and Ed. This exercise will enable you to see the world from Ed's point of view while at the same time you need not accept his anger and defensiveness. This is your chance to be an empathic leader enabling him to improve his skills and chances for success.

Coaching Session Notes

. . . .

. . . .

. . . .

. . . .

. . . .

. . . .

. . . .

. . . .

. . . .

. . . .

. . . .

Stages in the Empathic Interview

Although no empathetic interview can be conducted by following a script, here is an outline for you to consider as you picture empathizing with Ed and trying to make a difference in his life.

As you review the stages outlined below, apply them in your mind to the problem of coaching Ed, or try them out in a real-life coaching situation. If you are able to role-play this coaching opportunity with someone who can stand in for Ed, use the outline of stages to guide your coaching process.

Introducing the Session

Begin by creating an introduction to the conversation with Ed. Tell him why you are meeting with him and what you intend to achieve from the coaching session. Assume that he is willing to work with you, but because he is in character, also assume that he will be tough and let you know that he has all the answers figured out.

Setting the Stage

Create an opportunity for Ed to tell you what is wrong. As he speaks, empathize with his feelings. Try to see the situation from his point of view. Give him the opportunity to speak his mind and heart as you remain silent yet encouraging with nods and responsive body language.

Giving Empathic Remarks

Let him know that you can appreciate his situation and his feelings. Show him by summarizing his comments and acknowledging his emotions that you empathize with him. Do not buy in to his anger or defensiveness but encourage him to explore the issues further. Let him know you are with him in the search for a solution. Create a partnership with him.

Providing Supportive Feedback

Give Ed some honest feedback on his behavior and point of view and help him empathize with Baxter and the members of the Board. Let him know you have his self-interest *and* that of the company and its employees at heart. Empathy gives you permission to tell him honestly about the problems with his behavior. Do not protect him from himself. Be straight with him, but be supportive at the same time. Ask him if he is willing to try to improve his communication skills. If he resists, let him know again that you empathize by reflecting back to him some of his own comments, and find common ground. Encourage him to empathize with others and understand why his behavior has upset them.

Soliciting Reactions

Find out from Ed if he is receiving your feedback. Hear what he has to say and whether it is critical of you. If it is, use this as an opportunity to model for him how to accept criticism. Listen for his disappointment, pain, and sense of failure. Let him know you hear these feelings and that you can understand why he might feel that way. If you start getting lost in Ed's problems, reread Dr. Norman Paul's definition of empathy to center yourself.

Eliciting Changes

Help Ed create his own plan of action. Focus on the specifics of what he can do to change. Ask him to come up with a game plan for new behavior. Ask him to indicate the changes he would like to see in how others treat him. Prompt him to say what he will do differently in order to elicit new behavior and attitudes from others.

Offering Acknowledgment

Thank Ed for taking the risk of being open to himself and to you. Let him see how courageous he was when he became willing to change. Empathize with what it took for him to observe himself and identify the changes he will need to make to stimulate a different response from others. Encourage him to be more acknowledging of others and find little ways of complimenting them for work well done.

In earlier chapters we asked you to be self-reflective, and to learn from observing your reactions and behaviors. We would like you to use these skills again. Notice how you felt when you empathized with Ed. What problems did you have in identifying with him? What was it about him that triggered difficulties you had in understanding him? The discomfort you have can provide you with information about unresolved issues you may have with others or even with yourself. The buttons Ed pushed by his attitudes and behaviors may represent incomplete or unresolved concerns you have with yourself. These concerns can be your greatest teachers.

Here is an exercise you can try. On the left side of a piece of paper, make a list of the people with whom you are unable to empathize. Leave space between each name. On the right side of the paper, list the attributes of each person that you find disagreeable or that block your empathy with them. Now review the list of attributes and notice the similarities of those listed for each person. These attributes or characteristics may be ones you do not like in yourself, so you avoid them in others. If you want to be more successful in empathizing with others, you can examine and overcome these attributes or characteristics in yourself. By accepting them as part of your own makeup and finding ways of overcoming them, you will be able to tolerate them in another person. As a result of work on these issues, you will be able to empathize more easily with others and have more productive coaching relationships with them. Empathy is our greatest teacher about others and therefore about ourselves.

Ed's story highlights the power of our attitudes about our circumstances in shaping our view of ourselves and determining our behavior in becoming a leader. When we live and work in a world we cannot fully trust, as Ed did, we have a choice between three fundamental options. We can approach what happens that does not match our expectations with a *negative* attitude and treat it as a burden, or we can approach it with a *positive* attitude and affirm its beneficial features, or we can *transcend* both categories, reject them, and stop the ceaseless, complicated interplay between them.

In Joan's recent book with Ken Cloke, *The Art of Waking People Up: Cultivating Awareness and Authenticity at Work,* they explore the transcendent approach to leadership, which integrates the negative truth of harsh reality with the positive truth of generous possibility. Transcendence acknowledges the presence of necessity and opportunity, frustration and dedication, inadequacy and abundance, disaster and opportunity that are present in all change efforts. Leaders who transcend their circumstances do not accept the world as it is; rather, they work to transform it.

When we are negative or unhappy about life or its circumstances, it is easy to become apathetic or cynical and simply give up. When we are positive or happy, we easily become complacent and develop a stake in preserving the status quo. Either of these choices causes us to fix problems superficially or become dulled to the creative, transcendent possibilities that come from exploring the sources of negativity. Taking a negative approach to problems is useful in that it is the first step in recognizing the problem, but it is one that easily leads to cynicism and apathy, thereby disarming change efforts and perpetuating the problem. Taking a positive approach leads us to alternatives, but it can also promote denial of the importance of the problem and can result in superficial solutions.

When we recognize the higher, *combined* truth that lies hidden in both these alternatives, we start to recognize the deeper sources of our problems, shift them where they originate, and transcend the attitudes and ideas that got us into trouble in the first place. We can then move on to discover newer, higher orders of problems and generate more profound solutions. Taking a transcendent approach means seeing the problem in all its manifestations but not being discouraged by the seriousness or difficulty of the task ahead. At the same time, if we focus only on ourselves and ignore the external conditions that continually generate new problems, we will not succeed in overcoming them. We will merely escape the immediate need to face them and we will allow them to reappear in different guises. When we transform the systems that produced these problems and transcend our inner vulnerability to them, we more easily understand how we got into difficulty in the first place, how to collaborate in ending them, and how to avoid similar problems in the future. An enhanced commitment within ourselves to transcend the problem produces a determination to overcome it within the organization, or even in society as a whole. We become far more powerful and effective in solving problems when we have already solved them *within ourselves* and are able to approach them from a distant perspective; when we adopt an outlook that transcends negative and positive characterizations; when we create a context that is oriented toward the future and avoids getting stuck in the past.

Trust Through Consistency

The current disarray in corporations, church hierarchies, governments, and nonprofit agencies caused by revelations of fraud, corruption, theft, and betrayal has created an urgent need for leaders who are above suspicion and can be counted on to consistently adhere to moral, ethical, and value-based behavior.

The quagmire of inappropriate campaign contributions to candidates in exchange for favors in the political sector; the violation of honest audit practices by major accounting and auditing firms in the corporate world; the misuse of grants and donated contributions to nonprofit agencies; the cover-up of sexual abuse of minors by Catholic priests—all have stimulated an urgent demand for leaders we can trust.

Time magazine's cover story a few years back asked the right question: "What Ever Happened to Ethics? Assaulted by Sleaze, Scandals and Hypocrisy, America Searches for Its Moral Bearings." The editors went on to say:

> At a time of moral disarray, America seeks to rebuild a structure of values. . . . Large sections of the nation's ethical roofing have been sagging badly, from the White House to churches, schools, industries, medical centers, law firms, and stock brokerages—pressing down on the institutions and enterprises that make up the body and blood of America. At the same time, the collapse of standards brings ethical issues to the forefront. Many Americans feel a need to start rebuilding the edifice, to reevaluate the basis of public morality. In so doing, says Joseph Kockelmans, professor of philosophy at Pennsylvania State University, "people may finally begin to take responsibility for their lives, instead of just being sheep."

We have become numb to scandal and corruption in high places. Although it may not be condoned, it is often accepted, causing us to abandon our trust in leaders, leaving cynicism in its place. This country desperately needs leaders who uphold values against self-interest and consistently stand for moral and ethical integrity. How do we reestablish trust? We have to develop leaders who have a clear and compelling vision, consistently demonstrate empathy, and can be counted on to practice ethical behavior. It is consistent integrity that we are seeking, as well as courageous ethical action. We seek reliability, or what we prefer to call "constancy," in those who lead us.

A recent national study indicates that people would much rather follow individuals on whom they can count, even when they disagree with their viewpoint. They prefer leaders with ideas that are contrary to their beliefs to people with whom they agree but flip-flop in their positions or change willy-nilly. We cannot emphasize strongly enough the significance of constancy, of staying the course. A leader's regular and consistent pattern of integrity provides security and builds trust. In the long haul, strong moral and ethical values allow trust to fully blossom between a leader and followers. Leaders generate and sustain trust by exemplifying the following characteristics:

Constancy

The surprises leaders themselves face are not passed on to their followers. They maintain continuity and create security by being consistently ethical, even when their ideas and positions evolve to reflect changing circumstances.

Congruity

There is no gap between the theories that leaders espouse and the ones they practice. Their morality is found in their behavior.

Reliability

Leaders are there when it counts. They are ready to support their coworkers in the moments that matter.

Integrity

Leaders honor their commitments and promises. They are ethical in their relationships.

Harold Williams, former President of the J. Paul Getty Trust, clarifies this idea when he describes his early experiences as Chairman of the Securities and Exchange Commission (SEC):

> If there is anything I feel good about [at the SEC], it's the way I came through in terms of my own personal values and my personal self. If you believe in your course, you gotta stay with it in terms of course and timing. I think it's tough at times—when the press are all over you and you start hearing from Capitol Hill and you know that even some of your own staff are feeding the

stories and the corporate community is up in arms, and there were several times when it was all going that way and it gets kind of heavy. . . . But if you believe you're right, and you've got your own integrity—and I think that's where it really ends up—I mean: "Do you believe in what you're doing?"— And if you believe it you stay with it. I couldn't change course and still respect myself.

In our current organizational and political environment, the only constant is change, and a sense that the integrity, to which Williams points, is slowly disappearing. The dilemma for each of us is this: How can a leader maintain consistent commitments without seeming to be rigid and unresponsive to shifting realities? It is a fine line to walk in today's volatile climate to steer a clear and consistent course while empathizing with, responding to, and addressing constant change. Leaders are expected to acknowledge uncertainties and deal effectively with the present while simultaneously anticipating and responding to the future. This means endlessly expressing, explaining, extending, expanding, and, when necessary, revising the organization's mission as well as their own vision. Leaders can change their minds, but they need to be consistent in their values, which includes being open to change. They need to demonstrate this same value—constancy—in how they communicate these changes, how they behave in relation to change, and how they explain the thinking process that got them to a new position.

Thomas L. Friedman, writing in the *New York Times* about then President Bill Clinton, who had then been in the White House for one month, describes his problem of constancy as follows:

> How will Mr. Clinton respond when the screaming starts? One friend of Mr. Clinton compares him to a character in the television show "Star Trek: The Next Generation." The character is an "Empath," one of a race of people born with an ability to empathize with and absorb the feelings of others. As he prepares his economic program, the Empath President is clearly uneasy.

"More than anything else he doesn't want to anger people," said the friend. "He wants to be loved. He doesn't want to do things that will hurt people, but that is fundamentally incompatible with the Presidency."

In retrospect, it is clear that Clinton, like the rest of us, wanted to be loved. Staying the course, maintaining a consistent focus, and being predictable in terms of what a leader believes will not always end in his being loved, but it will lead to effective leadership and increased trust. Yet as the later stages of the Clinton presidency reveal, people soon begin to distrust a leader who does not consistently uphold the values he preaches or tell the truth about his mistakes.

We are not advocating that leaders take a position and stick to it no matter what. In today's organizations, which require flexible, responsive, innovative leadership, digging in one's heels and sticking to one's guns are strategies that are doomed to failure. But we *are* urging constancy in ethics, values, and integrity. Leaders are responsible for the ethics and norms that govern the behavior of people in their organizations. Leaders can lead through ethics and values in several ways. One is to demonstrate their commitment to the ethics and values they want to institutionalize by matching their own behavior with their values. Leaders set the moral tone in organizations by carefully choosing the people with whom they surround themselves, by communicating a sense of purpose to the organization, by empowering employees to articulate and live by their shared values, by reinforcing value-based behaviors, and by articulating strong ethical positions to external and internal constituencies. John Gardner, writing in *No Easy Victories*, describes a leader's role with regard to ethics and values as follows:

> Leaders have a significant role in creating the state of mind that is the society. They can serve as symbols of the moral unity of the society. They can express the values that hold the society together. Most important, they can conceive and articulate goals that lift people out of their petty preoccupations, carry them above the conflicts that tear a society apart, and unite them in pursuit of objectives worthy of their best efforts.

In the end, vision, empathy, constancy, and integrity are all different faces of leadership. If organizations are successful in creating ethical, value-based leadership, they can operate as a single organism that is in harmony with itself and comfortable in its environment.

Your Ethical Ten Commandments—An Exercise

One of the most powerful archetypes of a leader in Western culture is Moses, whose leadership was based on his ability to move people to action with a vision of freedom and personal responsibility. He was as troubled by the corruption of his time as we are today. His response was to deliver to his people the Ten Commandments, which provided a code of ethics, by which his followers could live to achieve their vision.

When we speak of a code of ethics, values, and integrity, we mean the standards of moral and intellectual honesty upon which our conduct is based. Without integrity we betray ourselves and others and cheapen every endeavor and all success. Integrity is the single quality most distinctly missing on every level of our national life. Our nation's integrity will be restored only when each of us asserts our individual integrity and becomes responsible for upholding values in our own lives. We do not need to wait for others to change. People of integrity, by their very existence, enable us to rise above the current cynicism and moral squalor.

The chronic rash of recent scandals we have faced is actually the result of *millions* of undiscovered, uncounted incidents of people cheating, evading, covering up, telling half-truths, and petty moral erosions, not only by our leaders but also by our own behavior and that of the "little people" in our society. The slogan for these seedy times might be, "But everybody does it!" Ethics, values, and integrity, like charity, begin at home.

In the following exercise, you are asked to take an honest look at your own code of ethics and values. Using the metaphor of the Ten Commandments, we invite you to write your own moral and ethical standards for your behavior. This will give you an opportunity to scan your belief systems, discover your values, and fine-tune the ethical code you want to use to guide the leadership behaviors of yourself and those of others. We ask you to focus on your own behaviors because the true test of a leader's integrity is his consistent expression of a code of ethics in everyday behaviors. Our ability to know what we believe and our commitment to live by those beliefs will enable us to succeed in creating relationships of trust with others.

We recommend that you work alone at first, then share your results with others. Complete the following charts by practicing self-reflection and observing your own behavior. On the first chart, you are asked to create your own Ten Commandments for ethics in your organization. These commandments are the ten most important values you champion for your work. On the second chart, you are asked to indicate concrete behaviors you have demonstrated that exemplify each commandment. For example, if one of your commandments is to "do no work that contributes to the loss of life of another human being," you might evaluate the products manufactured by your company to make sure there is no toxic waste being dumped where human beings could be harmed. If you have a commandment that says "never cheat the company out of money," you will want to check your expense reports for accuracy and honesty.

My Ten Commandments for Ethics on the Job

1. . . . .

2. . . . .

3. . . . .

4. . . . .

5. . . . .

6. . . . .

7. . . . .

8. . . . .

9. . . . .

10. . . . .

My Concrete Behaviors That Exemplify Each Commandment

1. . . . .

2. . . . .

3. . . . .

4. . . . .

5. . . . .

6. . . . .

7. . . . .

8. . . . .

9. . . . .

10. . . . .

After you have completed these charts on your own, share them with others to identify the similarities and differences that can exist in the same workplace. Next try to honestly answer the following questions to assess areas where you can improve.

Questions to Consider

A. What were your most strongly held values, and how did you express them?

B. Which commandments were least strongly held, or most difficult to use, in guiding your behaviors?

C. Were there any commandments that were important to you for which you could not find corresponding behaviors?

D. Would you and your colleagues be willing to give each other feedback about whether your behavior matches your commandments? If not, why not?

E. What have you and/or your colleagues noticed about each other's values, and the willingness of each of you to take a stand for your values?

F. How has your organization supported you in following your commandments, and how has it hindered you?

Bridging the Integrity Gap—An Exercise

There is often a gap between what we believe is right and the actions we take. Melissa Everett, Dr. John Mack, and Dr. Robert Oresick are authors of a study that addresses the stresses and conflicts faced by corporate executives in trying to increase company profit and improve products while remaining true to their moral, value, and ethical commitments. In their research report *Re-Inventing the Corporate Self: The Inner Agenda for Business Transformation*, they found two types of executives: those they called "principled risk-takers," and those they characterized as "conventional decisionmakers." They analyzed their interviews of twenty-four senior executives who worked in publicly held corporations and discovered differences in the following three areas:

1. **Self-Consistency: Wholeness or Compartmentalization**
   These individuals saw life as an integrated whole in which their beliefs applied consistently with church groups, volunteer organizations, and values at home.

2. **Personal Efficacy: High or Limited Sense of Agency**
   These individuals had a sense of power and control in their work life so that they believed they could take action to express their values.

3. Scope of Awareness: Global or Circumscribed

These individuals saw themselves as global citizens with responsibilities that are larger than their own corner of the world.

In this exercise, you will need a partner. Your partner's assignment is to interview you by asking questions that will enable you to discover whether you are, for the most part, a "principled risk-taker" or a "conventional decision-maker."

Although no one is completely one type or another and we are all combinations of both, it will be useful to notice your tendencies to favor one approach or the other. This exercise will also let you know where you stand in terms of your own "integrity gap," so you can make informed choices about your actions in relation to your commandments.

The interviewer begins by asking you the questions listed below. He will write down your responses and give them to you for analysis. *Do not* think long and hard about each answer, rather, respond quickly and accurately. When you have completed the interview, change roles and take on the role of interviewer. When you have both been interviewed, read over your responses and share your observations and reflections with each other.

Interview Questions

A. When you come to your job each day, do you feel you have to put aside ethics or values that are important to you in order to get along and be successful? If so, what are these ethics or values, and what makes you think you have to put them aside?

. . . .

. . . .

. . . .

. . . .

B. Have you ever experienced a situation at work when you knew the right action to take but felt you should or could not take it because it would not be accepted or valued? If so, please describe.

. . . .

. . . .

. . . .

. . . .

C. Are there times at home when you act consistently with ethics or values that you wish you could express at work? Are there feelings you have when you volunteer for a community organization or church group that you do not have at work but would like to have? If so, what are they?

. . . .

. . . .

. . . .

. . . .

D. Do you feel that you have the authority and power to act on beliefs that are important to you at work? If so, what actions have you taken to express your values? What happened as a result?

. . . .

. . . .

. . . .

. . . .

E. Are you aware of your organization's impact on the larger community and on the world as a whole? If so, is this impact positive, negative, or a complex picture? Please describe.

. . . .

. . . .

. . . .

. . . .

F. How does your work contribute to the improvement of your society, of people in other societies, and of the world as a whole? If you do not see a connection to the larger community, what impact does your work have on your local community?

. . . .

. . . .

. . . .

. . . .

G. Do you see yourself as a global citizen with responsibilities for people and events beyond your community and your country? If so, what are some examples of these responsibilities? If not, how do you see yourself relating to people and events in the world beyond your community?

. . . .

. . . .

. . . .

. . . .

When you and your partner have completed the interviews and the analysis of your responses, you may find you have created a picture of your integrity gap. The results of this exercise will indicate the changes you can make to live your values more fully in an integrated way. The ability to trust a leader grows directly out of the leader's consistent expression of ethics through communication and action. Dr. Martin Luther King Jr., in a letter written from a Birmingham, Alabama, jail where he was incarcerated for acting on his values in support of civil rights for all people in society, described the responsibility each of us has to live our beliefs through action:

> I am coming to feel that the people of ill will have used time much more effectively than the people of good will. We will have to repent in this generation not merely for the vitriolic works and actions of the bad people, but for the appalling silence of the good people. We must come to see that human progress never rolls in on wheels of inevitability. It comes through the tireless efforts and persistent work of men willing to be co-workers with God, and without this hard work itself becomes an ally of the forces of social stagnation. We must use time creatively, and forever realize that the time is always ripe to do right.

What actions do you need to take to become the kind of leader who can respond with courage to Dr. King's challenge? In Chapter 7 you will learn how to create a plan of action to increase the congruence between your values and your actions.

7 Realizing Intention Through Action

In all we do, we must affirm an unyielding moral vision—that the next gen-eration is entitled to participate fully in reinventing and benefiting from the American future. If we believe in ourselves, we will find and create a vital and participatory community in which every student, faculty, and staff member is valued and respected, in which we recognize that we share com-mon values as educated and ethical human beings, and in which the bonds of community are stronger than the habits of cultural ignorance. That is our fervent goal.

If we believe in ourselves, we will create the kind of learning environment and campus community that will prepare our graduates for a lifetime of learning, ethical conduct, global sensitivity, and service. Those institutions that will succeed in achieving a 21st-century version of academic excellence will be those institutions that believe—in their students, in their communities, in themselves—and as a consequence of that belief, will take risks and design radically new approaches to embracing the imperative of change.

Dr. Blenda Wilson, President, California State University–Northridge, Inaugural Address, April 30, 1993

OUR GENERATION FACES STAGGERING CHALLENGES. BLENDA WILSON'S call to us to leave a legacy of harmony and opportunity for the future will require responses of a different order and quality than those to which we have become accustomed. Everything you have learned in this workbook and more will be called upon to bail us out of our current morass and help us realize a new vision for the future.

Where will we find the leaders we need? The challenge before us is to recruit and sustain the most talented people possible and include them in the effort to create a future worth having. The first task of anyone who hopes to lead a successful organization is to find and inspire leadership worthy of the challenges we confront. The people who can achieve something truly unprecedented have more than enormous talent and intelligence. They have original minds. They see things differently. They can spot the gaps in what we think we know. They have a knack for discovering interesting, important problems, as well as the skills for solving them. They want to do the next thing, not the last one. They see connections. Often they have broad interests and multiple frames of reference. They tend to be deep generalists, not narrow specialists. They are not so immersed in one discipline that they can't find solutions in others. They are visionaries and problem-solvers before they are managers. They can no more stop looking for new relationships and better ways of doing things than they can stop breathing. They have the tenacity that is so necessary to accomplish anything of value. They are aware of what they are doing, and they bring an authenticity and integrity to the process. More and more of our workers are, to use Peter Drucker's decades-old phrase, "knowledge workers." Today we should add that more and more are "owner/investor workers," bringing their own profitable ideas into companies in which they invest and partly own.

But where will the leaders come from to run new organizations, to guide this emerging workforce, and to deliver a viable new economy? Organizations going for longevity need to discover continued sources of learning, growth, and revitalization. But how do we reach the next generation? Do we continue to do what we have been doing with just a little bit more? The discrepancy between the promise of available talent and the capability to deliver on their potential raises questions we need to consider. Are we providing learning experiences that will build the cognitive, emotional, and interpersonal competencies that are required for sustainable leadership in the "new economy"? Is there space in our clogged work lives for the philosophy, metaphysics, and critical thinking of the enterprise itself? Are we giving our employees a passion for continual learning, a refined, discerning ear for the moral and ethical consequences of their actions, as well as an understanding of the purpose of work and human organizations?

These are formidable questions. As we consider them we realize that it is an intense journey to achieve a positive sense of ourselves and recognize our abilities and limitations. We can get there by understanding what it takes for us to learn about ourselves: by learning to solicit and integrate feedback from others, by continually keeping ourselves open to new experiences and information, and by having the ability to hear our own voice and see our own actions.

A Self Assessment Prior to Action

In our work together we have clarified the essential qualities of leadership. We have affirmed that leaders:

1. Know themselves through reflection and self-observation;
2. Understand both their history and present environment;
3. Are clear about their values and goals;
4. Are aware of and can apply their learning style to solving problems;
5. Are willing to be lifelong learners;
6. Can take risks and are open to change;
7. Are able to accept mistakes and failures as necessary precursors to creativity and problem solving;
8. Are skilled in creating a vision and seeing themselves and their lives as part of this vision;
9. Are able to communicate their vision with meaning so that others are inspired by it;

10. Are committed to maintaining trust through empathy, constancy, and integrity; and

11. Are skilled in translating intention into reality through committed action.

Now is the time in our work together for you to take a moment to reflect on all that you have learned through the processes and exercises in this workbook. Each chapter of the book introduced and investigated a competency of leadership that we discovered as we interviewed, observed, coached, and mentored leaders of countless organizations, governments, agencies, and communities. We now want to give you an opportunity to assess your capacity to deliver on these competencies in your work and in your life.

The assessment instrument below provides a framework for you to use in measuring your strengths in each of the following six competencies of leadership. A leader who is competent:

    I. Masters the Context
   II. Knows Him/Herself
  III. Creates Visions for the Future
  IV. Communicates with Meaning
   V. Maintains Trust Through Integrity
  VI. Realizes Intentions Through Action

Please take a moment to review your work this far in relation to each of these components. You may want to look back over your comments in each chapter that address particular competencies with which you feel unsure. When you feel you have made the appropriate review of previous chapters and read forward in this chapter to understand more about the sixth competency by which a leader realizes her intentions through action, you will be ready to begin the Self Assessment.

As a first step, review the specific behaviors listed below for each competency. These behaviors describe the competency and indicate what leaders do to demonstrate their skill in each area.

Give yourself a rating for each item from 1 to 5.

1 = I do not demonstrate this competency.

5 = I am extremely successful in demonstrating this competency.

Note: This assessment is focused on your leadership in the workplace. If you are a student, retired, or unemployed, extrapolate the behaviors to your classes, home life, volunteer work, or community activities, and give yourself a rating for your leadership role in these non-work settings.

COMPETENCIES OF LEADERSHIP ASSESSMENT

1. Masters the Context

RATING	COMPETENCY	RECOMMENDATIONS
4	Is aware of the major issues in the larger environment and their impact on decisions.	
4	Critically synthesizes information from internal and external sources when solving problems.	
4	Encourages diverse input and perspectives when developing plans and making decisions.	
4	Considers possible outcomes and alternative actions when creating strategies.	
2	Takes calculated risks to change the organization.	*not any more*

2. Knows Him/Herself

RATING	COMPETENCY	RECOMMENDATIONS
5	Focuses on self-learning and developing a learning environment for all staff.	

4   Cultivates relationships and alliances with teams and leaders to meet employee needs.

3   Builds networks of colleagues to create professional learning communities.

3   Views errors and mistakes as learning opportunities for leadership development.

4   Participates regularly in staff development as a leader and as a learner.

3. Creates Visions for the Future

RATING   COMPETENCY   RECOMMENDATIONS

2   Has a clear vision and articulates it powerfully.

3   Pursues opportunities and develops strategies consistent with the articulated vision.

2   Helps individuals define personal visions and roles consistent with the organizational vision.

2   Revisits the organizational vision regularly to revise it and to align strategies to the vision.

3

Is able to let go of past
practices and expectations
to create the future from a
vision of the future.

4. Communicates with Meaning

RATING COMPETENCY   RECOMMENDATIONS

4

Practices empathetic listening
and honest dialogue with
colleagues.

4

Is willing to confront conflicts and
pursue resolution of all issues.

3

Is clear about one's own voice
and able to make it heard.

4

Seeks feedback and changes
behavior based on what is
learned.

4

Constructively uses disagreements
and conflicts to develop innovative,
collaborative solutions.

5. Maintains Trust Through Integrity

RATING COMPETENCY   RECOMMENDATIONS

4

Has clear values and communicates
them through commitments and
behavior.

3

Provides others with opportunities
to learn from mistakes and problems.

4

Values diversity and supports the
quality and quantity of diversity
in the organization.

4 Demonstrates behavior that is
   consistent with values, ethics,
   and standards for integrity.

3 Provides opportunities for others
   to demonstrate and expand
   their skills.

6. Realizes Intentions Through Action

RATING   COMPETENCY   RECOMMENDATIONS

4 Gets results and adds value
   to efforts by transforming
   strategies into action.

4 Assumes personal responsibility
   for improving organizational
   achievement.

3 Questions bureaucratic roadblocks
   and eliminates them.

4 Evaluates results to improve work
   processes.

4 Is able to credit others and publicly
   acknowledge their contributions.

After you have given yourself a rating for each of the items, it is time to step back and look at the whole picture you have created of yourself.

For each item in which you rated yourself a 4 or below, take a moment to consider what you might do to improve your skills. For each of these items, go back and make comments in the space provided on the right side of the page indicating what you can do to improve your capacity as a leader. Notice that there may be patterns of behavior that cut across the six competencies. Identify priorities for your continued development so you can give yourself a rating of 5-plus for each competency in the future.

This assessment should enable you to summarize the work on leadership that you have completed. It should also provide an outline for future activities as you engage leadership development as a lifelong learning process.

Formulating Your Intention

In preceding chapters, we have shared conceptual models, experiences of leaders, reflections by leaders on their encounters with life, and numerous exercises designed to develop your understanding and leadership skills. The insights you have gained will support you through a lifetime of learning. There is one more segment of our work together that remains to be completed. We now address the final competency of a leader: the ability to make it happen, to realize dreams, to translate intention into reality, to take action and produce results.

All action is predicated on having an intention, in which you know what you want and set out to achieve it. Some people are born knowing what they want and even how to do it. The rest of us are not so lucky. We have to spend time figuring out what to do with our lives. We are unaware of our intentions. Jamie Raskin, a former assistant attorney general in Boston, told us, "One of my heroes is a professor at Harvard Law School named Derek Bell. He told me that it's important not to have any specific ambitions or desires. It's more important to have ambitions in terms of the way you want to live your life, and then the other things will flow out of that." Derek Bell demonstrated this tenet in his own life by taking a leave of absence from the faculty at Harvard Law School until the school changed its hiring practices for faculty to include African-American women.

So what is it that you want to do with your life? The majority of us go though life without ever asking, much less answering, this basic question. The first step in becoming a committed and strategic leader is to know one's intentions and understand the relationship between your intentions and your skills; to know how to deploy your talents to achieve your goals. In order to prepare yourself to become a leader and a person of action, answer the following questions.

Questions to Consider

A. What do you want? What abilities or capacities do you have that could be useful in trying to get it? What is the difference between what you want and your abilities?

B. What drives you? What gives you satisfaction? What is the difference between what drives you and what satisfies you?

C. What are your values and priorities? What are the values and priorities of your organization? What are the differences between your values and your organization's priorities?

D. Recognizing the differences between what you want and what you are able to do, between what drives you and what satisfies you, and between your values and your organization's priorities, what might you do to overcome these differences?

Because a basic human drive is to express one's self fully, effective action must be based on self-expression. However, if there is a gap between what you want to achieve and your ability to reach your goal, between what gives you satisfaction and what drives you, or between what is important to you and the values of your organization or the larger society in which you live, you will become frustrated and feel powerless unless you create an *intention* to use your leadership skills to enlist others in the effort to achieve your goals.

If we assess our wants against our capabilities, the issues are fairly basic. Almost every one of us has, at some point in our lives, wanted to be an NFL quarterback, a Nobel Prize–winning scientist, a jazz singer, a movie star, but we simply did not have the requisite equipment. Although it is possible to learn anything, certain occupations require gifts that are beyond learning. We know a highly successful radiologist, for example, who has always dreamed of being a jazz singer but has no voice. Instead of abandoning her dream, she writes songs.

A would-be quarterback who is fast and smart but weighs only 140 pounds might well become a coach or organize a Saturday afternoon touch-football league among friends and coworkers.

When we distinguish between satisfaction and drive, the issue becomes more complex. We all know people who are driven to succeed—never mind at what or how—but who are never satisfied and remain unhappy all their lives. It is entirely possible to succeed and satisfy yourself simultaneously, but only if you are wise enough and honest enough to know what you want and feel satisfied when you have done everything you can to achieve it.

If your values and those of your organization differ, you can learn a lesson from the case of Ed, presented in Chapter 6. If he had thought more clearly about what he wanted and what his company needed, he would not have driven himself off the career track by focusing his intention on the wrong goals. He spent all his energies *doing* things and proving himself rather than *being* a leader and letting his authenticity win the favor of those in power. Some corporate cultures are so rigid that they require absolute obedience to the corporate line. Others are more flexible, adjustable, and adaptable. Knowing the degree of flex in yourself and in the organization in which you work will either help you create a better fit, or enable you to find an organization where you can.

Clarity about your goals, awareness of your sources of satisfaction, and commitment to your values are necessary precursors to taking action. Understanding where your goals and those of your organization differ will allow you to make more informed and strategic choices.

Your Goals Statement—An Exercise

A wise proverb reminds us that if we do not know where we want to go, any road will take us there. In order to act effectively, it is wise to be clear about our goals. Having a vision of what we want is a beginning. But without clear goals that can be measured, communicated, and acknowledged when achieved, it is possible to roam in circles. In Chapter 2, when we discussed how to use this book, we asked you to create long-term and short-term goals for your growth as a leader. At this point, we encourage you to revisit this earlier work and see how your goals have changed as you have evolved through your work in succeeding chapters.

Because this chapter represents the end of our learning process together, we would like you to build on your work in previous chapters. In particular, please refer back to the visions you created for your organization and your own life in Chapter 5. If your perspectives have changed, create new visions now using the tools we gave you in Chapter 5.

With your vision in place, review your goals as a leader and create five or six goals you would like to achieve in your work during the next year that will bring you closer to achieving your vision. Here are the steps to use in creating your goals:

Steps in Setting Goals

A. Project an image of yourself one year from now and picture where you will be, how you will feel, and what you will be doing. Try to picture what it will be like to realize your vision.

B. Now identify the five or six key accomplishments you will have achieved by that point. Limit yourself to five or six goals. More than six may be overwhelming, and fewer than five goals may not be comprehensive enough to make a difference.

C. Your goals should be objectively measurable and identifiable so you and others will know when you have achieved them.

D. Your goals should directly support your vision and move your organization toward your vision.

Using these 4 steps, complete the chart below, listing your goals. Begin by referring to your vision, then create goals to support that vision. We will refer to this chart throughout the rest of the exercises in this chapter.

My Vision for My Organization Is:

The 6 Goals I Will Achieve in One Year That Will Support Me in Realizing My Vision

1. . . . .
2. . . . .
3. . . . .
4. . . . .
5. . . . .
6. . . . .

If you are working in a team or with a partner, share your goals and ask for feedback. Ask an outside observer if your goals seem to support your vision. Do they seem to be achievable in one year? Are they worth accomplishing, worth the effort? Do you notice any overlaps or similarities to the goals of others in your organization? If so, can you find ways to support one another?

Now that you know what you want and have your vision and goals in place, it is appropriate to clarify your commitment and desire to meet them.

Commitment and Desire Are Requisites for Action

It is not easy to bring a dream into reality. Without commitment and desire, no action is likely to be effective. There are many stumbling blocks in the road, many minefields laid by others, many failures waiting to discourage you. You will prevail only if you have a deep and profound commitment to your vision and your goals, as well as a strong desire to fuel your behavior and make them real. Many people we know take heart from the following statement. We often see it hanging on the wall in offices and homes. It speaks to commitment on all levels for all endeavors.

Until one is committed
there is hesitancy, the chance to draw back,
always ineffectiveness.
Concerning all acts of initiative (and creation),
there is one elementary truth,
the ignorance of which kills countless ideas
and splendid plans:
that the moment one definitely commits oneself,
then Providence moves too.
All sorts of things occur to help one
that would never otherwise have occurred.
A whole stream of events issues from the decision,
raising in one's favour all manner
of unforeseen incidents and meetings
and material assistance,
which no man could have dreamt
would have come his way.
    *   *   *

I have learned a deep respect
for one of Goethe's couplets:
    *   *   *

"Whatever you can do, or dream you can, begin it.
Boldness has genius, power, and magic in it."
    *   *   *

W. H. Murray, *The Scottish Himalayan Expedition*

The type of commitment Murray describes can lead to a range of achievements from personal goals to conquering the peaks of the Himalayas. When we speak of commitment, we are talking about "stick-to-it-iveness" and persever-ance. Commitment requires a combination of focus and attention. As we gain purpose with commitment, we may also experience a sense of loss that is asso-ciated with the choices we did not make. When one is committed to a course of action, a specific person, or a set of goals, we give up searching for alternatives. Our commitments call for a single-mindedness that draws us away from other choices.

Having commitments can also be embarrassing. In many organizational cul-tures, it is the norm to be noncommittal, to hedge your bets, play your cards close to the vest, check out the trends, and clear it with the powers-that-be be-fore making a move. With commitment comes self-revelation and increased vulnerability. When one is committed, one acts according to one's deepest prin-ciples and strongest ideals, realizing it is always possible to fail. But for a leader, increasing the strength of your commitment is a form of success in itself.

Desire is a close and necessary partner to commitment. Without passion or desire, our commitments are dry and do not enliven or improve anyone—in-cluding ourselves. Desire is a natural response; it exists in all of us. Virtually every one of us was born with a hunger for life, and with it comes a passion for the promises of life. That passion can take us to the heights. Unfortunately, in too many of us, it can also turn into an addictive drive that takes us to the depths. Entrepreneur Larry Wilson defined the difference between desire and drive as the difference between expressing yourself and proving yourself. In a perfect world, everyone would be encouraged to express themselves passion-ately and no one would be required to prove themselves, but neither the world nor we are perfect.

Passions and Commitments—An Exercise

Often we are not conscious of our commitments and passions until they are ex-pressed in our behavior or until they are challenged by someone else. Often we

189

are unaware of what we care about until we act, and in the process of acting we discover our passions. When we are not conscious of our convictions, we are unable to be strategic or win others to our side, and we may even alienate potential supporters. In the following exercise, we ask you to become aware of your passions and explore their origins so you can claim them and use them more fully to guide your leadership behaviors and enlist the support of others.

Steps in Recognizing Your Passions and Commitments

A. On the chart provided below, create a chart of your life passions, the things you feel intensely about. Notice which ones were unconscious before this exercise. Which commitments did you discover? Which ones were conscious and which were unconscious? Is there a pattern you can discern?

B. Which passions do you usually express openly? Which ones are more private? How does your family, your organization, and your social circle support or block the expression of your passions? Are there any passions you want to express more consistently in your work?

C. Which passions are part of your identity? Share your list with someone who knows you well. Would they be able to guess your passions? Discuss their perceptions of your passions and learn more about how others see you.

D. On the chart for passions below there is a space next to the area in which you will list each passion. In this space indicate the origin of this passion. Is it something you learned in your family, or did you emulate it from a mentor or friend? If so, indicate who taught it to you and how they expressed it. Is it something you created? If so, describe the experience in which you developed or adopted this passion. What do you notice about the origins of your passions? Is there a pattern for how you choose your passions?

E. If you are working with a team, share your passions and their origins. Notice the range of passions expressed in the team and how they are expressed by each of you. Discuss how all members of the team can be supported to more openly express and live by their passions. Discuss how you can bring your passion into the work environment more successfully.

Passions Chart

True Passions   *Origin*

. . . .

. . . .

. . . .

. . . .

. . . .

. . . .

. . . .

. . . .

. . . .

. . . .

As a next step in this exercise, please refer back to your vision and reexamine the goals you generated earlier. Revealed in your vision and goals are your commitments and passions. In this exercise, we ask you to analyze your vision and goals in order to highlight your commitments. For example, if you have a vision of a truly diverse workplace, and a goal of increasing diversity in your organization by 30 percent in one year by making sure that at least one candidate for every vacated position is a qualified person of color, then people will recognize that you are a leader who is committed to diversity in the work environment.

Review your vision and goal statements. In the space provided below, list as many commitments as you can identify that are embedded in your vision and goals. Do not censor any ideas. This is a personal brainstorming process. Even if some commitments seem outlandish or extreme, write every one of them down.

. . . .

. . . .

. . . .

. . . .

. . . .

. . . .

. . . .

. . . .

. . . .

. . . .

Now review your list. Were you surprised by any of the commitments on your list? Which ones are your true commitments? On which ones would you stand or fall? Where is your passion with regard to these commitments? Why there?

Commitments and passions come from the heart. But leaders must work both strategically—from the mind—to create ideas and they must work passionately—from the heart—in order to create effective action. Strategic thinking is the next skill needed for you to improve your leadership capacity. Without a strategy to guide your action, without an overall plan, you will be reduced to guesswork, trial and error, and a series of passionate failures.

Strategic Thinking

There is an old saying: "Unless you are the lead dog, the scenery never changes." To extend that thought: For the leader, the scenery is always changing, everything is new, because each leader who is out in front is by definition unique, and the scenery, whatever it is, will be perceived uniquely. In response to the chaos of our times comes a demand for leaders to be strategic thinkers. A well-developed strategy allows leaders to think creatively and come up with solutions to problems that have not yet even been manifested. A strategy is what takes a leader out of the reactive mode; it provides a demand for creativity and initiative. The capacity for strategic thinking is one of the intangible traits of leadership that is difficult to teach. Sydney Pollack, when asked if leadership could be taught, responded:

> It's hard to teach anything that can't be broken down into repeatable and unchanging elements. Driving a car, flying an airplane—you can reduce those things to a series of maneuvers that are always executed in the same way. But with something like leadership, just as with art, you reinvent the wheel every single time you apply the principle.

Creativity and strategy are inextricably interconnected. The creative process that underlies strategic thinking is infinitely complex, yet there are basic steps in creative strategic planning that make the process accessible. While the following five steps may not be linear or required, they can guide you in developing an effective strategy to realize your vision and achieve your goals.

First, whether you are planning a novel or a corporate reorganization, you need to know where you are beginning and where you want to end up. Mountain climbers start climbing from the bottom of the mountain. They look at where they want to go and work backward to their starting point. Like a mountain climber, once you have the summit in view, you can plan all the best ways of getting there. As you plan your strategy, you will need to assess your choices—altering, connecting, compromising, revising, imaging—and finally you will choose one route to get where you want to go, with a backup in case the first one fails. We continue the mountain-climbing analogy as we take the next steps in strategic thinking.

Second, you will explore these routes, elaborate them, revise them, and map them out, so they are complete with notations of possible pitfalls and traps, as well as rewards that wait along the way.

Third, you will determine whether the direct route is the most sound, or whether you should make a more cautious, circuitous approach.

Fourth, you will plan the resources you need and the means by which you will go about securing them. You will also identify the allies who can assist you in this effort.

Fifth, you will examine your map objectively, looking at it as if you were not its maker. You will then be able to locate all its soft spots or danger points and eliminate or change them to highlight the route that is most secure.

Finally, when you have finished creating your strategy, you will harness your passion and commitment—and set out to climb the mountain.

A good example of the way a leader can deploy a strategy to succeed was reported by our colleague, Frances Hesselbein. Together with her husband and their families, she lived in Johnstown, Pennsylvania, for four generations. They had a communications business, and she worked as a Girl Scout volunteer. As a volunteer she did management training for Girl Scout councils around the country. When she was asked to take over the CEO slot of the local council temporarily, she agreed. Six years later, though she had not applied for the job, she was made Executive Director of the Girl Scouts of America. She and her husband moved to New York City and she set about reorganizing the Girl Scouts to reflect everything she had learned on her way up the ladder. She described her experiences this way:

> The first thing we did . . . was to develop a corporate planning system in which planning and management were synonymous. It was a common planning system for 335 local councils and the national organization. We developed a corporate planning monograph to mobilize the energy of 600,000 adult volunteers in order to carry out our mission to help young girls grow up and reach their highest potential as women. Today, our people feel we've achieved more unity and cohesion than anyone can remember.
>
> I just felt there was compelling need to . . . have a clear planning system that defined roles, differentiating between the volunteers, and the operational staff, and the policy planners, one that permitted whatever was going on in the smallest troop—needs, trends, whatever—to flow through to the policy makers, so they had a clear idea of what was going on and what needed to go

on. We have three million members, and we really listen to the girls and their parents, and we've devised ways to reach out to the girls wherever they are. We say, "We have something of value to offer you, but you in return have something to offer us. We respect your values and culture, and if you open our handbooks, even if you are a minority, a Navajo, you're there." The best thing about it is that every girl in America can look at the program and see herself.

Hesselbein had a vision to create a responsive, inclusive organization. Her strategy was to use planning to move the Girl Scouts organization in that direction, and she was successful in applying her strategy to realize her vision and achieve very specific, concrete goals for her organization.

The Strategy Map—An Exercise

The concept of strategy originated in the military. It grew out of the need to achieve an advantageous position through the movement of troops, supplies, and ammunition, if possible, without alerting the enemy. Using strategy in an organization, however, need not require a conflict or the intention of defeating an enemy in order to achieve one's goals. Strategies are driven simply by a need to achieve something that is desired and may not be easily or readily achievable. Strategies take into consideration many variables, including human relations, politics, and social factors as well as costs, materials, and logistics. You need not apply a military command-and-control style to implement a strategy. The leaders we admire are able to include others in creating their strategies and carrying them out. The most successful strategic leaders behave as the ancient Chinese philosopher Lao-tzu described:

Fail to honor people,
They fail to honor you;
But of a good leader, who talks little,

When his work is done, his aim fulfilled,
They will all say, "We did this ourselves."

In the exercise below, we ask you to create a strategy map. To do this, you will need to select one goal from the list of five or six you identified earlier.

A. Pick a goal you would actually like to reach and write it below:

. . . .

. . . .

. . . .

In order to create a strategy map, you will need to think of your goal as both a journey and a destination. It is somewhere that you would like reach, and it is also the way you intend to reach it. You will need to identify a starting point. For example, in working with the goal we articulated of increasing diversity, there may be several starting points. Perhaps only 1 percent of your staff is represented by people of color, so qualified minority applicants are reluctant to even apply. Perhaps your personnel department is not enthusiastic about recruiting suitable candidates. Perhaps you do not know how many positions will be available this year. Perhaps you don't know how to monitor the advertisement of openings, interviews, and other aspects of the hiring process to make certain they are fair and unbiased. Finally, you may not know how to contact the talent pool that could be asked to fill the positions. To create your strategy you will need to know your starting point.

B. Identify the starting point for achieving your selected goal, from which you will mount your strategy:

. . . .

. . . .

. . . .

. . . .

. . . .

To create your strategy map, you will need to have a clear assessment of the allies on whom you can count and the resources at your disposal. In our example, you would need to know who in the personnel department could be more receptive to achieving your goal. You might have to do a cost analysis of the plan to identify the financial resources available, as well as those whom you will need to help in launching the recruitment effort. You might also identify other organizations that have achieved similar goals and recruit allies from their ranks. In other words, for the strategy to be successful, you will need to know who are your allies, what resources you have at your disposal, and what is needed to get where you are going.

C. List your potential allies:

. . . .

. . . .

. . . .

. . . .

D. List the resources you have available, in addition to those that are needed to be successful:

. . . .

. . . .

. . . .

. . . .

Now it is time to create your strategy map. The map is a visual representation of your strategy. Strategies are high-level tools. They are not specific actions, tactics, or behaviors. They give you a fallback position to which you can always return if a particular action, tactic, or behavior is not successful. Without a strategy, if your tactic fails, you might give up completely. If you have a strategy and a particular tactic does not work, then you can return to the strategy, regroup, and invent another tactic.

For example, our strategy to reach our goal of increased diversity might be to involve the personnel department, with a tactic of brainstorming ways to attract more minority applicants. If this is our strategy and our brainstorming effort bombs, we do not need give up. Our strategy is not to brainstorm with them; it is to get them involved. So we can analyze the meeting, learn from our mistakes, and try another tactic. This new tactic might be to meet individually with each person to identify our natural allies before going back to the department as a whole. Our strategy keeps us on course and focused on our goals at all times.

Using the model on the following page, create a Strategy Map for achieving your goal. In the lower left-hand corner identify your starting point, and in the upper right-hand corner write your goal. Map A shows a straightforward example. Connect the starting point and the goal with a line. If your strategy is direct, the line will be straight, connecting the two points by the shortest possible route, as shown in Map A. If you have to take a more circuitous route, your strategy will look more like Map B.

Now include your allies and the resources that you have available or those that you will need in order to reach your goal. You may show these supportive elements in your strategy as indicated in Maps A and B. Place your allies above the line and your resources below it. This picture will give you a clearer idea of your strategy and how you can support it.

If you are working with others, you may want to draw your maps on large pieces of flipchart paper or on a whiteboard. Otherwise, you can use the strategy map worksheet we have provided. Share your strategy map with colleagues and ask for a reality check from them. Do your colleagues agree with your list of

Strategy Map

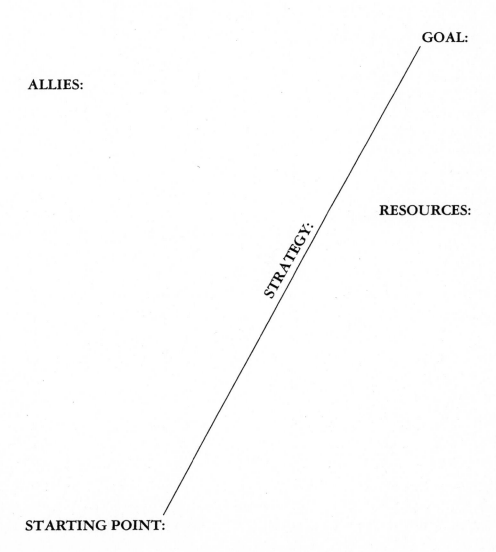

GOAL:

ALLIES:

RESOURCES:

STRATEGY:

STARTING POINT:

Map A

GOAL:
Positions Filled with
People of Color

ALLIES:

Other Organizations with Experience

Executive Managers who
Support the Goal

Line Managers Who Want
to Hire People of Color

Individuals in Personnel
Who Support the Goal

STRATEGY:
Have the Personnel Department Own the Goal and Commit to Achieving It

RESOURCES:

Travel Money for Candidates
for Positions

Funds for Special Recruitment

Recruiters and Head Hunters
with Good Contacts

Funds for Special Meetings
to Create Buy-in for Goal

STARTING POINT:
1 Percent of Staff Are
People of Color

Map B

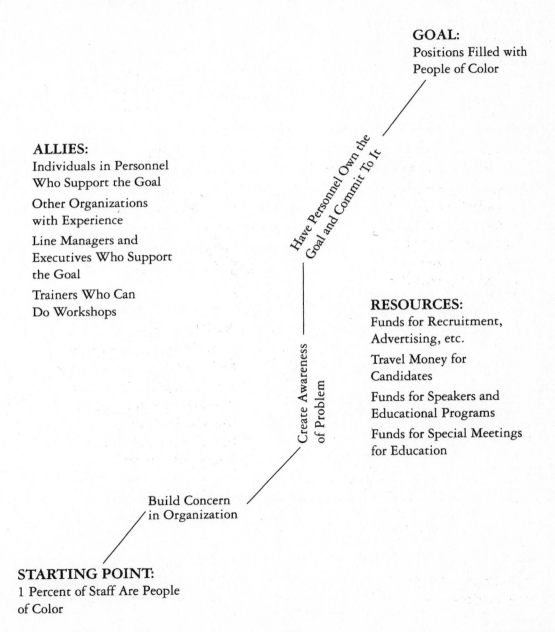

GOAL:
Positions Filled with
People of Color

Have Personnel Own the
Goal and Commit To It

ALLIES:
Individuals in Personnel
Who Support the Goal

Other Organizations
with Experience

Line Managers and
Executives Who Support
the Goal

Trainers Who Can
Do Workshops

RESOURCES:
Funds for Recruitment,
Advertising, etc.

Travel Money for
Candidates

Funds for Speakers and
Educational Programs

Funds for Special Meetings
for Education

Create Awareness
of Problem

Build Concern
in Organization

STARTING POINT:
1 Percent of Staff Are People
of Color

allies and resources? Have you created the most powerful strategy? What are the likely obstacles, pitfalls, and dangers in pursuing your strategy? Are they willing to support you? How will you support them?

Power to Achieve Your Goals—Exercises

No discussion of leadership, or of how leaders translate visions into reality, would be complete without a brief reference to power. We often associate power with physical force, but it is a more complex dynamic than the show of military might. With coercive power, there is usually either a tangible reward for compliance or a penalty for noncompliance. It is a relatively simple transaction that is based on a relationship of physical, mental, or emotional coercion. Power can also come from identification with the people or ideas that are the sources of perceived power. Followers emulate the leader with whom they identify and blindly carry out his or her bidding.

A third type of power comes with expertise. The person on the receiving end either respects or seeks to attain the same level of knowledge as that of the expert, who becomes a leader by virtue of their superior knowledge or skill. There is also group power, in which the members of a group conform by following the norms of the culture. There is power based on access, in which people, goods, and decisionmaking authority become available through personal contacts. There is the power of persuasion, in which the follower is won over to a side or point of view through an argument or convincing demonstration.

The usefulness of each type of power depends on the goal, the starting point, and the strategy you are employing. For example, if you are mounting a strategy based on involving the personnel department in increasing diversity in hiring, it would be counterproductive to employ a coercive form of power. That would only result in "public compliance and private defiance," as some employees have called it. Instead, we suggest using an inspiring, empowering, leadership strategy so that our goal is owned by the department and they give full commitment to achieving it. However, if you were conducting a training program on diversity, you could use the power of your expertise and hope the participants would gain a knowledge of the importance of diversity. You might also encourage them to emulate you through the power of identification with your ideas.

Kareem Abdul Jabar, the former star forward of the Los Angles Lakers basketball team, wrote of empowering leadership in his autobiography. He ascribes this leadership to his coach at UCLA, John Wooden, who gave him his start and empowered him in his early years:

> As a competitor, he was unnerving. Many coaches in the then Pac 8 [conference] didn't like him because he was too good to be believed. He wanted to win, but not more than anything. Coach Wooden wanted to win very much, but within the rules, within the guidelines he had set for the expression of his own and his players' competitive talent. Within those, he went all out. He understood the game totally. He eliminated the possibility of defeat. It was genius. . . . I don't know why fate placed me in his hands, but I'm grateful that it did. My relationship with him has been one of the most significant of my life. He believed in what he was doing and what we were doing together. He had faith in us as players and as people. He was about winning basketball and winning as human beings. The consummate teacher, he taught us that doing the best you are capable of is victory enough, and that you can't walk until you can crawl, that gentle but profound truth about growing up.

How have you experienced, expressed, or used power in your own life? Your history with power, as it was practiced toward you and as you have used it, could significantly influence your choice of the form of power you might use as a leader. In the next exercise, you will explore experiences with different types of power that can be used to achieve a goal. You will have an opportunity to identify the types of power you have used and the limits and opportunities they provided. This activity of self-reflection will allow you to become conscious of your use of power and enable you to choose the form of power that will be most successful for you as a leader.

On the chart below we have listed the types of power we distinguished earlier. Remember a time when you used each type of power or experienced it being used to achieve a particular result. Describe the incident briefly, then reflect on the positives and negatives, and the limits and opportunities, provided by the use of that form of power.

TYPE OF POWER	INCIDENT	LIMITS	OPPORTUNITIES
Coercive			
. . . .			
. . . .			
. . . .			
Identification			
. . . .			
. . . .			
. . . .			
Expert			
. . . .			
. . . .			
. . . .			
Group			
. . . .			
. . . .			
. . . .			

204

Access

. . . .

. . . .

. . . .

Persuasion

. . . .

. . . .

. . . .

Inspiration and Empowerment

. . . .

. . . .

. . . .

When you have completed your chart, share it with your colleagues. Ask yourself these questions: Did you find one form of power more limiting than others? Did you have examples of the use of these different forms of power from your organization? Which forms of power are reinforced in your organization, and which are discouraged? What would have to change in your organization for inspiration and empowerment to be the most frequently used form of power?

As you reflect on your experience, think about how comfortable you feel with each form of power, both as a leader and as a follower. What would it take for you to make inspiration and empowerment the main form of power deployed to achieve your goals? As you ready yourself to make your vision a reality, consider empowerment as the expression of your power and find ways of empowering others to choose and support your goals.

Write a scenario below in which you use empowerment to achieve your goals. You may have to reconsider your strategy in order to incorporate a more inclusive, inspiring, and empowering approach. Include in the scenario details about how you will enact your strategy, who will be involved, how you will inspire and empower them, what their behaviors will look like, and what results you will achieve.

A Scenario for Achieving Your Goals Through Inspiration and Empowerment:

. . . .

. . . .

. . . .

. . . .

. . . .

. . . .

. . . .

. . . .

. . . .

. . . .

. . . .

. . . .

. . . .

. . . .

. . . .

. . . .

. . . .

. . . .

. . . .

. . . .

. . . .

Inspiration and Empowerment: A Conclusion

Inspiration and empowerment reflect the qualities of leadership that lie at the heart of this workbook and are most important in learning to lead. In organizations with effective leaders, inspiration and empowerment are most evident in four characteristics of work life that are initiated, supported, and sustained by leaders. When these four exist, organizations are successful and leaders feel fulfilled. We offer them as a final reflection on leadership and as you complete this course and start your journey as a lifelong leader.

Characteristics of organizations in which leaders lead through inspiration and empowerment are:

People feel significant. Everyone in the organization feels that in some way they make a difference to the success of the organization. Where there is inspiration and empowerment, people feel their work matters and that what they do has meaning and significance.

Learning and competence matter. Leaders value learning, and so do the people who work for them. Leaders make it clear that there are no failures—only mistakes that give feedback and indicate what to do next.

People are part of a community. Where there is true leadership based on inspiration and empowerment, there is teamwork and unity. Everyone has a chance to be recognized and heard. When the team works beautifully, it feels like a loving family.

Work is exciting. Where there are leaders who inspire and empower, the work is stimulating, challenging, fascinating, and fun. Empowering leaders articulate and embody the ideals toward which their organization strives. Members of these organizations enroll themselves in visions that are attainable, and their behaviors exemplify their ideals through committed action.

Quality is valued. In an inspired and empowered organization, quality is one of the supreme values held by all. Quality may not always be measured, but it is appreciated intuitively. Feelings of quality are intimately connected with our experience of meaning and beauty and values in our lives.

Dedication produces results. Closely linked to the concept of quality is dedication. Dedication is evoked by quality and is the attracting force that energizes high-performance systems. When we love our work, when it has quality, we do not have to be managed by rewards or fears of punishment. We can create systems that facilitate our work to produce results of which we are proud.

When these aspects of organizational life are achieved, we see a distinct, dramatic change take place in the philosophy underlying organizational behavior. A new concept of humanity is called forth. This new concept is based on expanded knowledge of our complex and shifting needs, replacing the oversimplified, innocent, push-button idea of humanity. This philosophical shift calls for a new concept of organizational values based on humanistic-democratic values and ideals, which replace the depersonalized, mechanistic system of bureaucracy. With it comes a new concept of power, one based on inspiration and empowerment, collaboration and reason.

The challenge each of us faces is to be able to express and foster in others the leadership skills that can enable them to achieve these goals and build more collaborative, democratic, inspired, and empowered work lives and, as a result, families, communities, and societies that are worth having.

We hope you will continue to develop and improve on these ideas and implement all that you have begun in the learning partnership we have shared. Inspiration and empowerment lead us ultimately to love ourselves, our work, and our lives. More we cannot wish you.

ACKNOWLEDGMENTS

If we were to acknowledge all the leaders in our lives, the ones who inspired us to write about leadership and the ones who challenged us to be more than we are, we would have a list of names that would match this book in size—and then some. We could fill another volume with the many students and colleagues from whom we have gathered ideas and with whom we have shared activities. Some of these women and men *are* named in the text. They are quoted and noted as their lives provide examples for the learning experiences presented here. Because we are not able to tell you of all our heroes and teachers in the time or space we have, we hope they know who they are and we hope they will accept our thanks for their inspiration and teachings.

We want especially to thank our partners in life, Grace Gabe and Ken Cloke, for their love and light. Near the very end of our revisions, Ken Cloke brought his loving editorial pen to our final draft. We thank him for contributing his elegant language to this volume. Our assistants Lisa Miller, Grace Silva, and Solange Raro deserve special acknowledgment for doing what it took to produce this workbook. We thank Laura Campobasso for her leadership in creating a valuable bibliographic resource. Thanks to our editors, William Frucht and Nick Philipson. Their contributions made the process of bringing the workbook to publication smooth and satisfying. Finally we want to thank Miriam Goldsmith for her loving proofreading and much more.

A BIBLIOGRAPHY OF RESOURCES ON LEADERSHIP DEVELOPMENT

by Laura Campobasso and Daniel Davis

1. Arendt, Hannah, *Origins of Totalitarianism*, Peter Smith Pub., 1983.

    A comprehensive history of totalitarianism, from the rise of anti-Semitism in Central and Western Europe in the 1800s through the institutions and operations of Nazi Germany and Stalinist Russia.

2. Athos, Anthony, and Pascale, Richard, *The Art of Japanese Management*, Warner Books, 1982.

    A comparison of Japan's Matsushita Electric Company and ITT, concluding that the fundamental differences between U.S. companies and their Japanese competitors lie in managerial style and cultivated skills rather than in organizational structures or systems.

3. Badaracco, Joseph L. Jr., *Leading Quietly: An Unorthodox Guide to Doing the Right Thing*, Harvard Business School Press, 2002.

    An argument that most of the world runs off the sum of the many small, seemingly unimportant daily decisions made by "quiet leaders" who avoid the limelight to focus on responsible, low-key action to resolve difficult challenges.

4. Barnard, Chester Irving, *The Functions of the Executive*, Harvard University Press, 1971.

    The first book to provide a comprehensive theory of cooperative behavior in formal organizations, analyzing the psychological and social factors that both motivate and impede cooperation.

5. Bass, Bernard, *Bass and Stogdill's Handbook of Leadership*, Free Press, 1990.

    A reference book, providing brief but thorough summaries of leadership research and thought.

6. Bennis, Warren G., and Thomas, Robert J., *Geeks and Geezers: How Era, Values, and Defining Moments Shape Leaders*, Harvard Business School Press, 2002.

    A comparison of today's young leaders with those of their grandparents' era, concluding that "crucibles"—utterly transforming challenges and tests—either break or embolden potential leaders.

7. Bennis, Warren, and Nanus, Burt, *Leaders: The Strategies for Taking Charge*, 2nd Ed., HarperBusiness, 1997.

Through extensive interviews with business and public-sector leaders, the authors identify two common attributes of leaders: (1) the ability to give vision to their organizations, and (2) the ability to translate those visions into reality.

8. Bennis, Warren, *On Becoming a Leader*, 3rd Ed., Perseus, 2003.

The author elaborates six key principles supporting the thesis that the two essential components of leadership are creating a vision and translating that vision into reality.

9. Bennis, Warren, and Biederman, Patricia Ward, *Organizing Genius: The Secrets of Creative Collaboration*, Addison-Wesley, 1997.

Rather than focusing on individual leaders, the authors examine "Great Groups," synergistic collaborations that have left an enduring legacy, and argue that the Great Group and its great leader create each other.

10. Bennis, Warren; Spreitzer, Gretchen M.; and Cummings, Thomas G., Editors, *The Future of Leadership: Today's Top Leadership Thinkers Speak to Tomorrow's Leaders*, Jossey-Bass, 2001.

A comprehensive collection of essays from today's foremost writers on leadership. Topics include the role of ethics in contemporary leadership, who is "responsible" for leadership, and why bad leaders are tolerated.

11. Bennis, Warren, *Why Leaders Can't Lead: The Unconscious Conspiracy Continues*, Jossey-Bass, 1989.

Bennis attributes leaders' inability to take charge and lead to an unconscious conspiracy in contemporary society and offers new insights and a more clearly developed conceptualization of the failures of present-day institutions.

12. Bolman, Lee G., and Deal, Terrence E., *Leading with Soul: An Uncommon Journey of Spirit*, Jossey-Bass, 2001.

A perspective on leadership as a modest, intensely personal journey, requiring self-knowledge and the humble attitude of a servant/leader. The book addresses such current issues as the changing workforce, the changing nature of work itself, and the need for "soul" in the workplace.

13. Bossidy, Larry, and Charan, Ram, *Execution: The Discipline of Getting Things Done*, Crown Business, 2002.

The authors argue that the key to closing the gap between promised and actual results is being passionately engaged and fostering dialogues based on intellectual honesty and realism. They posit that one of a leader's most important jobs is choosing key people to create an "execution culture."

14. Buckingham, Marcus, and Clifton, Donald O., *Now, Discover Your Strengths: How to Develop Your Talents and Those of the People You Manage*, Free Press, 2001.

The book identifies thirty-four positive "personality themes" and describes how to build a "strengths-based" organization by reinforcing and leveraging strengths already present in the organization's human capital.

15. Burns, James McGregor, *Leadership*, HarperCollins, 1985.

A study of the history, theory, and practice of leadership, distinguishing between *transforming leadership*, which shapes and elevates the motives and goals of followers, and *transactional leadership*, which mobilizes resources to realize goals held by both leaders and followers.

16. Cloke, Kenneth, and Goldsmith, Joan, *Thank God It's Monday! 14 Values We Need to Humanize the Way We Work*, Irwin Professional Publishing, 1997.

A call for a more humane and fulfilling work environment. The authors focus on practical organizational change and offer exercises to help integrate the title's 14 Values into the workplace.

17. Cloke, Kenneth, and Goldsmith, Joan, *The Art of Waking People Up: Cultivating Awareness and Authenticity at Work*, Jossey-Bass, 2003.

A description of new ways of utilizing feedback to foster individual and organizational change, based on the belief that organizations should develop systems, processes, techniques, and relationships that affirm the intelligence and humanity of their employees.

18. Cloke, Kenneth, and Goldsmith, Joan, *The End of Management and the Rise of Organizational Democracy*, John Wiley & Sons, 2002.

The authors call for a radical set of organizational development initiatives that will enable companies to produce high-quality, competitive products in a workplace environment characterized by values, ethics, and integrity, and utilizing processes that are more humane and environmentally sustainable.

19. Conger, Jay A., and Benjamin, Beth, *Building Leaders: How Successful Companies Develop the Next Generation*, Jossey-Bass, 1999.

This book studies the experience of a variety of organizations, identifies three dominant approaches to leadership education, and provides a framework for organizations to apply them to cultivate leaders on an ongoing basis.

20. Conger, Jay A.; Spreitzer, Gretchen M.; and Lawler, Edward E. III, Editors, *The Leader's Change Handbook: An Essential Guide to Setting Direction and Taking Action*, Jossey-Bass, 1998.

The USC Leadership Institute and the Center for Effective Organizations convened some of the nation's top business theorists to present cutting-edge thought on leadership and change management.

21. Conner, Daryl R., *Leading at the Edge of Chaos: How to Create the Nimble Organization*, Jossey-Bass, 1998.

The book addresses the organizational and human elements required for an organization to be nimble and able to adapt instantly to today's changes, including rapid globalization, technological innovation, and increasing pressure from shareholders.

22. Covey, Stephen, *The 7 Habits of Highly Effective People*, Running Press, 2000.

The author asserts that true success is a function of both personal and professional effectiveness and focuses on practical application of new habits to achieve individual change.

23. Davenport, Thomas H., *The Attention Economy: Understanding the New Currency of Business*, Harvard Business School Press, 2001.

The author describes attention as a critical and scarce resource and presents six basic units of attention-related "currency" that companies use to capture and hold people's attention.

24. DePree, Max, *Leadership Is an Art*, Doubleday, 1989.

The author explores how executives and managers can build better, more profitable organizations by creating covenantal relationships where people are enabled to meet corporate needs through meeting one another's needs.

25. Dotlich, David L., and Cairo, Peter C., *Unnatural Leadership: Going Against Intuition and Experience to Develop Ten New Leadership Instincts*, Jossey-Bass, 2002.

The book explores the complex problems facing today's leaders and posits a nexus between strong character and strong leadership.

26. Eccles, Robert G., and Nohria, Nitin, with James D. Berkley, *Beyond the Hype: Rediscovering the Essence of Management*, Harvard Business School Press, 1992.

Discusses the role of the individual manager in mobilizing organizational action and effectiveness, focusing on action, identity, and rhetoric as the keys to connecting words and action.

27. Ellis, Joseph J., *Founding Brothers: The Revolutionary Generation*, Alfred A. Knopf, 2000.

An argument that the highly personal interactions of key Revolutionary War figures formed the foundation of the new republic, including similarities and differences in beliefs and goals that persist in our political discourse today.

28. Follett, Mary Parker, et al., Editors, *Mary Parker Follett—Prophet of Management: A Celebration of Writings from the 1920s*, Harvard Business School Press, 1996 (out of print).

A collection of lecture essays written or given between 1925 and 1933 on such topics as authority, leadership, the role of the individual in groups, and the place of business in society.

29. Freud, Sigmund, *Group Psychology and the Analysis of the Ego of Sigmund Freud*, W.W. Norton & Co., 1974.

Freud viewed individual and group psychology as inextricably linked, if not identical. This work examines the emotional bonds that bind groups together.

30. Gardner, Howard, with Emma Laskin, *Leading Minds: An Anatomy of Leadership*, Basic Books, 1995.

   A cognitive framework for leadership asserting that effective leaders share four characteristics, based on a study of eleven twentieth-century leaders as diverse as Margaret Mead and Mahatma Gandhi.

31. Gardner, John W., *On Leadership*, Free Press, 1989.

   A comprehensive analysis of leadership concepts, including such aspects as power, motivation, commitment, leaders and followers, shared values, and institution renewal. The author discusses and distinguishes among leadership, status, and power.

32. George, Bill, *Authentic Leadership: Rediscovering the Secrets to Creating Lasting Value*, Jossey-Bass, 2003.

   The author believes that true leaders must have a purpose and understand why they are leading and outlines five important leadership qualities: purpose, values, relationships, self-discipline, and heart.

33. Gergen, David R., *Eyewitness to Power: The Essence of Leadership, Nixon to Clinton*, Simon & Schuster, 2000.

   Based on the author's experience in a series of political administrations, this book examines what it takes to be a great political leader and describes seven leadership qualities of a great president; also applicable to leaders in other contexts.

34. Gladwell, Malcolm, *The Tipping Point: How Little Things Can Make a Big Difference*, Little, Brown & Co., 2000.

   The author compares mass behavioral change to epidemics and identifies dynamics that cause events by generating critical mass, or "tipping points," attributable to minor alterations in the environment and the actions of a small number of people.

35. Goleman, Daniel, *Emotional Intelligence*, Bantam Books, 1997.

   The author argues that traditional IQ measurements are narrow predictors of success and that "emotional intelligence" is a better indicator of human success.

36. Goleman, Daniel; McKee, Annie; and Boyatzis, Richard E., *Primal Leadership: Realizing the Power of Emotional Intelligence*, Harvard Business School Press, 2002.

   This work posits that leaders' actions account for 70 percent of employees' perceptions of their organizations and argues for "resonant leadership," which is built on emotional intelligence and results in leadership styles based on collaboration and inspiration.

37. Grove, Andrew, *Only the Paranoid Survive: How to Exploit the Crisis Points that Challenge Every Company and Career*, Currency/Doubleday, 1996.

   An argument that correct management of the "strategic inflection point"—a moment of massive change that requires an organization to adapt or fail—propels companies and individuals to greater success.

38. Hackman, J. Richard, *Leading Teams: Setting the Stage for Great Performances*, Harvard Business School Press, 2002.

    The author argues that team success depends on the leader's ability to structure a team, so that the members manage themselves, and identifies key conditions to increase the likelihood of success.

39. Handy, Charles B., *Age of Unreason*, Harvard Business School Press, 1991.

    The author describes profound developments in education, technology, business, and employment and argues that new kinds of thinking and organizations are required in order to turn these changes to our advantage.

40. Handy, Charles B., *The Age of Paradox*, Harvard Business School Press, 1995.

    This book identifies unintended consequences of intended change and describes guiding principles for coping with the challenges and paradoxes of modern life.

41. Handy, Charles, *The Elephant and the Flea*, Harvard Business School Press, 2002.

    A personal memoir acknowledging capitalism's possibilities and failures. The author describes the movement away from reliance on large companies to reliance on self, requiring creativity and agility.

42. Heenan, David A., and Bennis, Warren, *Co-Leaders: The Power of Great Partnerships*, John Wiley & Sons, 1999.

    A study of successful partnerships comprised of a dominant individual and a "number-two" person. The book argues for the importance of good lieutenants willing to forgo the spotlight to support an organization's success.

43. Heider, John, *The Tao of Leadership: Lao Tzu's Tao Te Ching Adapted for a New Age*, Humanics/New Age, 1985.

    The author draws on principles in the *Tao Te Ching* to offer inspiration and advice on how to develop as a leader.

44. Heifetz, Ronald A., *Leadership Without Easy Answers*, Belknap Press of Harvard University Press, 1994.

    Heifetz's model of leadership is a social contract where constituents confer power and resources in return for leadership and guidance.

45. Heil, Gary; Bennis, Warren; and Stephens, Deborah C., *Douglas McGregor, Revisited: Managing the Human Side of the Enterprise*, John Wiley & Sons, 2000.

    The authors apply the work of McGregor, MIT professor and one of the first business thinkers to focus on human capital, to current business realities and needs. Topics include motivation, commitment, cooperation, and performance.

46. Hill, Linda A., *Becoming a Manager: How New Managers Master the Challenges of Leadership*, Harvard Business School Press, 2003.

    Managers succeed by learning how to lead rather than doing the work themselves. The book follows nineteen new managers through their first year to reveal the complexities of transition to management.

47. Kanter, Rosabeth Moss, *E-Volve! Succeeding in the Digital Culture of Tomorrow*, Harvard Business School Press, 2001.

    The author posits that the Internet-driven "e-culture" is the core of the "new economy" and describes what organizations must know and do to incorporate the principles of e-culture into their business.

48. Kanter, Rosabeth Moss, *The Change Masters: Innovation and Entrepreneurship in the American Corporation*, Simon & Schuster, 1985.

    The author asserts the importance of incorporating entrepreneurial principles and practices in organizations as a way of creating flexibility engendering innovation to manage change effectively.

49. Kanter, Rosabeth Moss, *When Giants Learn to Dance: Mastering the Challenges of Strategy, Management, and Careers in the 1990s*, Simon & Schuster, 1989.

    The author argues that truly innovative organizations led the way in the turbulent 1990s, with the "giant" corporations shedding bureaucratic cultures and joining the postentrepreneurial "dance."

50. Keegan, John, *The Mask of Command*, Viking, 1987.

    The author studies four great military leaders to identify those qualities that inspired their followers, sometimes to victory and sometimes to defeat.

51. Kellerman, Barbara, *Re-Inventing Leadership: Making the Connection Between Politics and Business*, State University of New York Press, 1999.

    The author looks at the similarities between political and business leadership and argues that business and political leaders must work together to solve the most challenging social, economic, and political problems.

52. Khurana, Rakesh, *Searching for a Corporate Savior: The Irrational Quest for Charismatic CEOs*, Princeton University Press, 2002.

    In recent years, corporations have pursued charismatic individuals for their reputation and personality rather than experience and skills, artificially narrowing the pool of potential candidates, raising compensation, and increasing the likelihood of failure.

53. Kotter, John P., *A Force for Change*, Free Press, 1990.

    Kotter uses questionnaires and detailed case studies for insights into how corporations work. He distinguishes between managers, who execute by monitoring results against the plans, and leaders, who execute by motivating and inspiring people to overcome bureaucratic hurdles.

54. Kotter, John P., *The Leadership Factor*, Free Press, 1988.

    Kotter discusses the need for leadership at all levels of management. He considers how business is changing and the impact of these changes on leadership, makes recommendations, and discusses how to implement the recommendations.

55. Kotter, John P., *Leading Change*, Harvard Business School Press, 1996.

    The author argues that, for change to succeed, behaviors need to be altered. He describes common mistakes that prevent success and suggests eight steps for avoiding them.

56. Kotter, John P., and Cohen, Dan P., *The Heart of Change: Real-Life Stories of How People Change Their Organizations*, Harvard Business School Press, 2002.

    In this follow-up to *Leading Change*, the authors argue that companies often focus on changing how employees think about change, rather than how they feel. They introduce the "see-feel-change" process that inspires people to change their emotions by showing them powerful reasons for change.

57. Kouzes, James M., and Posner, Barry Z., *Credibility: How Leaders Gain and Lose It, Why People Demand It*, Jossey-Bass, 2002.

    The authors argue that leadership is based on relationship, and that relationship is dependent upon credibility. They offer six key disciplines and practices to strengthen a leader's ability to create and sustain credibility.

58. Kouzes, James M., and Posner, Barry Z., *Encouraging the Heart: A Leader's Guide to Rewarding and Recognizing Others*, Jossey-Bass, 2002.

    The authors believe that employees perform best when they are encouraged and their efforts appreciated. They argue that "compassionate supervision" is becoming a critical part of management today and that the appreciation must be real, demonstrated with rewards, and tied to standards of excellence.

59. Kouzes, James M., and Posner, Barry Z., *The Leadership Challenge: How to Get Extraordinary Things Done in Organizations*, Jossey-Bass, 2002.

    The authors draw from interviews with 500 managers to build and illustrate a model of leadership, covering such topics as identifying and developing leadership qualities and turning commitment into action.

60. Nohria, Nitin, *Driven: How Human Nature Shapes Our Choices*, Jossey-Bass, 2002.

    The authors present a sociobiological theory of motivation, claiming that humans possess four basic drives: to acquire, to bond, to learn, and to defend. Successful organizations give their employees opportunities to fulfill all of these drives.

61. Leavitt, Harold J., *Corporate Pathfinders: Building Vision and Values into Organizations*, Dow Jones–Irwin, 1986.

    This model of the management process involves three steps: pathfinding (asking the right questions); problem-solving (analysis); and implementing (action).

62. Lipman-Blumen, Jean, *Connective Leadership: Managing in a Changing World*, Oxford University Press, 2000.

    Increasing global interdependence requires "connective" leaders, who can move among various styles as the situation requires, and who have a superior feel for interdependence and an eye for diversity.

63. Lukacs, John, *Five Days in London: May 1940*, Yale University Press, 1999.

A historical account of the period immediately preceding Winston Churchill's decision that Britain would fight Germany, chronicling Churchill's perseverance in the face of wide opposition.

64. Machiavelli, Niccolo, *The Prince*, 2nd Ed., trans. Harvey C. Mansfield, University of Chicago Press, 1998.

Considered by many to be the definitive translation.

65. Maslow, Abraham H., *Maslow on Management*, John Wiley & Sons, 1998.

A highly influential writer on psychology and counseling, Maslow was widely known for his "hierarchy of needs." This book is the result of a journal written in 1962 when Maslow was hired to help give workers a voice in organizing production.

66. McCall, Morgan W., and Hollenbeck, George P., *Developing Global Executives: The Lessons of International Experience*, Harvard Business School Press, 2002.

The authors posit that the success of global businesses depends upon the quality of international executives developed through global experience. They highlight the key requirements and challenges of global leadership and emphasize the importance of experienced mentors.

67. McCall, Morgan W.; Morrison, Ann M. Lombardo, Michael M.; and Lombardo, Michael W., *Lessons of Experience: How Successful Executives Develop on the Job*, Simon & Schuster, 1998.

The authors interviewed senior executives in order to learn what experiences had the greatest impacts on their careers and what lessons were learned. They identify elements that maximize skill development and provide tools for evaluating the learning value of job assignments, as well as for creating jobs with higher development potential.

68. McCauley, Cynthia D.; Moxley, Russ S.; and Van Velsor, Ellen, Editors, *The Center for Creative Leadership Handbook of Leadership Development*, Jossey-Bass, 1998.

A comprehensive manual for individuals and organizations, describing the key elements of leadership development, focusing on six approaches to leadership development and providing tools to help organizations evaluate their efforts.

69. Meyerson, Debra, *Tempered Radicals: How People Use Difference to Inspire Change at Work*, Harvard Business School Press, 2001.

A book about reconciling personal and corporate ideals and agendas. The title refers to "quiet change advocates," individuals who seek to "fit in without selling out."

70. Miller, Arthur, *On Politics and the Art of Acting*, Viking Press, 2001.

One of the country's most prominent playwrights argues that the modern media have raised the level of acting ability required for political office; compares modern politicians from FDR to Clinton.

71. Nanus, Burt, *The Leader's Edge*, Contemporary Books, 1989.

    The author argues that leadership has been too preoccupied with the present at the expense of the future and the internal environment at the expense of the external one. He describes seven interrelated "mega-skills" required to correct these faults.

72. O'Toole, James, *Leadership A to Z: A Guide for the Appropriately Ambitious*, Jossey-Bass, 1999.

    An anthology of real-life stories with topics including communication, effectiveness, and listening.

73. O'Toole, James, *Leading Change: Overcoming the Ideology of Comfort and the Tyranny of Custom*, Jossey-Bass, 1995.

    The author posits that only value-based leadership is powerful enough to break through the inertia of comfort and custom to overcome the pull of the modern world's many distractions.

74. Palmer, Parker J., *The Courage to Teach: Exploring the Inner Landscape of a Teacher's Life*, Jossey-Bass, 1997.

    The author argues that good teaching is founded on the teacher's strong identity and integrity. Good teachers connect their students, their material, and themselves, enabling students to develop their own understanding of the world.

75. Pascale, Richard T., *Managing on the Edge: How the Smartest Companies Use Conflict to Stay Ahead*, Simon & Schuster, 1990.

    Pascale argues that modern management must embrace disequilibrium and transcend the old focus on control, stability, and avoidance of ambiguity.

76. Peters, Thomas, and Waterman, Robert, *In Search of Excellence: Lessons from America's Best-Run Companies*, Warner Books, 1988.

    A classic book on management. The authors identify and examine successful American companies and synthesize eight principles for success.

77. Pfeffer, Jeffrey, and Sutton, Robert I., *The Knowing-Doing Gap: How Smart Companies Turn Knowledge Into Action*, Harvard Business School Press, 1999.

    The authors argue that there is a gap between what many companies know they should do and what they actually do. They identify why companies fail to apply hard-earned knowledge and experience and suggest ways to create action.

78. Reich, Robert, *The Future of Success*, Knopf, 2001.

    The author analyzes the "new economy" and its impact on individuals' work and lives and proposes ways to create a more balanced society and more satisfying lives.

79. Rosen, Robert, with Brown, Paul B., *Leading People: Transforming Business from the Inside Out*, Viking, 1995.

    The book describes eight principles of leadership, illustrated with profiles of thirty-six of America's current notable leaders, and argues that the best, most effective leaders pay at least as much attention to principles and people as they do to profits.

80. Sample, Steven B., *The Contrarian's Guide to Leadership*, Jossey-Bass, 2002.

    A university president, the author offers insights and suggestions on leadership that often run counter to conventional wisdom.

81. Schein, Edgar H., *Organizational Culture and Leadership*, 2nd Ed., Jossey-Bass, 1992.

    An organization's culture lies in shared assumptions, and a leader must decipher these assumptions. Ultimately, the leader must foster a "learning organization," which contains the cultural mechanisms to manage and diagnose itself.

82. Schein, Edgar H., *The Corporate Culture Survival Guide*, Jossey-Bass, 1999.

    The author describes corporate culture as the "learned, shared, tacit assumptions on which people base their daily behavior" and argues that the failure to address them is an important reason that many corporate acquisitions fail.

83. Senge, Peter M., *The Fifth Discipline: The Art and Practice of the Learning Organization*, Doubleday/Currency, 1990.

    The author proposes the "systems thinking" method to help a corporation to become a "learning organization," one that integrates at all personnel levels in differently related company functions to improve productivity.

84. Snook, Scott A., *Friendly Fire: The Accidental Shootdown of U.S. Black Hawks over Northern Iraq*, Princeton University Press, 2000.

    The author approaches the event from individual, group, organizational, and cross-level perspectives and employs a rigorous analysis based on behavioral science theory to account for critical links in the causal chain of events.

85. Sonnenfeld, Jeffrey, *The Hero's Farewell: What Happens When CEOs Retire*, Oxford University Press, 1998.

    How a company deals with a CEO's replacement usually has a profound impact on the company's future. The author identifies four major types of departure styles and outlines suggestions for smooth leadership transitions.

86. Spears,, Larry C., and Lawrence, Michele, Editors, *Focus on Leadership: Servant-Leadership for the Twenty-first Century*, Jossey-Bass, 2001.

    A collection of essays on servant-leadership by prominent thinkers on leadership and management.

87. Tichy, Noel, and Cardwell, Nancy, *The Cycle of Leadership: How Great Leaders Teach Their Companies to Win*, HarperBusiness, 2002.

    Teaching and learning are the crux of effective leadership, and strong leaders foster both dynamics at all levels of the organization. This book provides specific information and strategies to guide organizations to build and maintain themselves as "teaching organizations."

88. Tichy, Noel, *The Leadership Engine: How Winning Companies Build Leaders at Every Level*, HarperBusiness, 1997.

   Organizations succeed when they have "good leaders who nurture the development of other leaders at all levels of the organization." The "leadership engine" created by this attention creates good leaders throughout the organization, all driving the organization in the same direction.

89. Tuchman, Barbara, *The March of Folly: From Troy to Vietnam*, MacMillan Library Reference, 1984.

   A Pulitzer Prize–winning author examines folly in governments throughout history. She defines "folly" in this context as a government's pursuit of policies contrary to its own interests, despite the presence of viable alternatives.

90. Useem, Michale, *The Leadership Moment: Nine True Stories of Triumph and Disaster and Their Lessons for Us All*, Crown Publishing Group, 1999.

   Nine dramatic stories about leaders in various fields and their responses to critical challenges.

91. Wills, Garry, *Certain Trumpets: The Nature of Leadership*, Simon & Schuster, 1995.

   Examines leadership as a mutually determined exchange between leader and follower. This concept is illustrated with sixteen biographies illustrating leadership in particular contexts.

92. Wren, J. Thomas, *The Leader's Companion: Insights on Leadership Through the Ages*, Free Press, 1995.

   A comprehensive collection of writings on leadership by a wide variety of experts and philosophers, from classic selections by Aristotle, Machiavelli, and Tolstoy to essays by modern experts such as James MacGregor Burns and Bernard Bass.

93. Yukl, Gary A., *Leadership in Organizations*, Prentice-Hall, 1981.

   A clear summary of basic issues for the new student of leadership. Topics include power and leader effectiveness, role, expectancy and adaptive-reactive theories, and determinants of effective group decisions.

REFERENCES

Preface

xi Peggy Dulany, unpublished essay "Why Some People Hate Americans."

xiii Charles Handy book review "It's Curtains for Managers" in *Management Today,* March 2002.

xiv Jimmy Carter "As a Citizen of a Troubled World" Nobel Prize for Peace Lecture Speech as reported in the *New York Times*, December 11, 2002.

Chapter 1

3 Sidney Rittenberg, personal communication with Joan Goldsmith, August 14, 1993.

7 Harlan Cleveland, *The Knowledge Executive*, E. P. Dutton, New York, 1985.

8 John W. Gardner, *On Leadership*, The Free Press, New York, 1990.

Chapter 2

27 Norman Lear, in Warren Bennis, *On Becoming a Leader*, Perseus, Cambridge, Mass., 2003.

Chapter 3

47 Jean Lipman Blumen, "Why Do We Tolerate Bad Leaders? Magnificent Uncertitude, Anxiety and Meaning," *The Future: Today's Top Leadership Thinkers Speak to Tomorrow's Leaders*, Jossey-Bass, San Francisco, 2001.

48 David Barboza, "The Meter Runs on Enron Case as the Lawyers Retain Lawyers," *New York Times*, December 25, 2002.

71 *Franz Kafka Diaries*, ed. Max Brod. Schocken Books, New York, 1948–49.

75 Susan Griffin, *A Chorus of Stones*, Doubleday, New York, 1992.

Chapter 4

82 Max DePree, *Leadership Jazz*, Doubleday, New York, 1992.

98 John Cleese, "No More Mistakes and You're Through," *Forbes*, May 16, 1988.

103 David Hare, *New York Times*, Sunday, November 10, 1991.

109 John Sculley, "Sculley's Lessons from Inside Apple," *Fortune*, September 14, 1987.

112 Arnold Hiatt, "Building Corporate Character: An Interview with Stride Rite Chairman Arnold Hiatt," *Harvard Business Review*, March-April, 1992.

113 Will Schultz, *The Human Element*, Jossey-Bass, San Francisco, 1980.

Chapter 5

120 George Bernard Shaw, *Man and Superman*, Penguin Books, Baltimore, 1973.

122 Barbara Corday, in Warren Bennis, *On Becoming a Leader*, Perseus, Cambridge, Mass., 2003, page 156.

122 Don Ritchey, in Warren Bennis, *On Becoming a Leader*, Perseus, Cambridge, Mass., 2003, page 157.

123 Frank Dale, in Warren Bennis and Burt Nanus, *Leaders: The Strategies for Taking Charge*, Harper & Row, New York, 1985.

132 Arlene Blum, *Annapurna, A Woman's Place*, Sierra Club Books, San Francisco, 1980.

133 Beth Jandernoa, *From the Leadership and Mastery Course* by Innovation Associates, Beth Jandernoa and Alain Gauthier, Framingham, Massachusetts.

138 Senator John Tunney, quoted in *New York Times*, June 7, 1989.

140 Marshall Frady, "Profiles: Jesse Jackson, Part II," *New Yorker*, February 10, 1992.

Chapter 6

143 Charles Handy, "What's a Business For?" *Harvard Business Review*, December 2002.

150 Sydney Pollack, in Warren Bennis, *On Becoming a Leader*, Perseus, Cambridge, Mass., 2003.

151 Norman Paul, "Parental Empathy" in *Parenthood*, E. James Anthony and Therese Benedek, eds., Little, Brown, New York, 1970.

161 Joan Goldsmith and Kenneth Cloke: *The Art of Waking People Up*, Jossey-Bass, San Francisco, 2003.

164 Harold Williams, in Warren Bennis and Burt Nanus, *Leaders: The Strategies for Taking Charge*, Harper & Row, New York, 1985.

165 Thomas L. Friedman, *New York Times*, Sunday, February 14, 1993.

166 John Gardner, "The Antileadership Vaccine" in *No Easy Victories*, Annual Report of the Carnegie Corporation, New York, 1965.

173 *A Testament of Hope: The Essential Writing of Martin Luther King, Jr.*, ed. James Melvin Washington, Harper & Row, San Francisco, 1986.

Chapter 7

175 Dr. Blenda Wilson, Inaugural Address, President, California State University Northridge, April 30, 1993.

183 Jamie Raskin, in Warren Bennis, *On Becoming a Leader*, Perseus, Cambridge, Mass., 2003, page 123.

188 W. H. Murray, *The Scottish Himalayan Expedition*, J.M. Dent & Sons Ltd., London, 1951.

193 Sydney Pollack and Robert Dockson, in Warren Bennis, *On Becoming a Leader*, Perseus, Cambridge, Mass., 2003, page 134.

194 Frances Hesselbein, in Warren Bennis, *On Becoming a Leader*, Perseus, Cambridge, Mass., 2003, page 135.

195 Lao-tzu, in Warren Bennis and Burt Nanus, *Leaders: The Strategies for Taking Charge*, Harper & Row, New York, 1985.

203 Kareem Abdul Jabar with Mignon McCarthy, *Kareem*, Random House, New York, 1990.

INDEX

blackboard
1poll68324
Luciadir09